Fearless Fai

Sally ыаск

© 2014 Vacationkids

Published 2015

ISBN: 978-0-9909108-0-0 Soft cover

Library of Congress Control Number: 2015901798

The author may be contacted at

Vacationkids.com, Inc. Publishing

Mom@Vacationkids.com

www.facebook.com/fearlessfamilyvacations

Covers and illustrations:

Angie Cleary & Jared Lewis

Printed in the USA

Table of Contents

Acknowledgements.. 5

« Introduction » 8

« Chapter One »...1

Different Kind of Travel Book..1

This Is Not a Typical Family Travel Book 2

« Chapter Two » 6

This Mom's Story 6

« Chapter Three » 14

Six Steps For Planning The Perfect Family Vacation 14

1.   WHO will be going on Vacation?...................................19

Travel Personalities 24

2.   WHEN will you be going?... 28

3.   WHAT TYPE of vacation does your family want?...........31

4.   WHERE do you want to go? 34

5.   HOW MUCH Is Our Vacation Budget? 36

6.   WHY Take This Vacation – Why Now?.......................... 40

« Chapter Four » 44

Travel Agents As Partners 44

« Chapter Five » 58

Six Stages of Family Vacations Through the Ages.................. 58

Pregnant Moms..61

Flying When Pregnant 63

Cruising While Pregnant.. 64

Hotels for Pregnant Moms... 65

Travel Tips for Pregnant Moms 66

Vacations with Baby... 68

Getting Started 69

Flying with Your Baby 73

Airport Security with a Baby 78

Car Seats 80

Strollers 81

Choosing the Right Hotel 83

Dressing and Packing for Baby.......................... 86

Swim Diapers.. 87

Sun Protection 89

TRAVELING WITH TODDLERS (ages 2–4)........................ 91

Flying with Toddlers..94

Toddlers in Hotels 95

Cruising with a Toddler.......................................98

Toddlers in Theme Parks.....................................99

School-Age Kids (ages 5–10).. 102

Family Vacations and the School Calendar 105

Tweens (ages 10–12) 108

Social Balance 108

WiFi or Unplugged Family Vacations 109

Independence and Safety 109

Teens (ages 13–18)... 111

Drinking Laws 112

Meals.. 112

Packing 113

Traveling without Family 113

The "Last" Family Vacation 114

Growing Families.. 115

« Chapter Six ».. 117

Real World Family Vacation Planning............................. 117

BIG FAMILIES 119

SINGLE PARENT vACATIONS 122

DIVORCED FAMILIES...127

BLENDED FAMILIES 131

GLBT FAMILY VACATIONS 134

MULTI-GENERATIONAL VACATIONS AND FAMILY
REUNIONS..138

    Group Discounts 141

THE EVOLUTION OF FAMILY VACATIONS......................145

« Chapter Seven »...147

SIX TYPES OF FAMILY TRIPS 147

FAMILY VACATION PACKAGES........................149

ALL-INCLUSIVE FAMILY RESORTS 153

Family Cruises 165

    Cruising with Baby...168

    Cruising with Toddlers....................................172

    Swim Diapers 173

    Kid's Clubs, Tweens and Teens 174

Escorted Tours..176

Theme Parks 181

    Disney...182

Family Adventure Vacations................................187

« Final Note » 191

Acknowledgements

Wow! If you've stopped to read this you're my kind of person. We're going to get along just great! I'll bet you're the type that sits to read movie credits too. I like your style.

Admittedly, childbirth was far less painful for me than having to sit down and write this book. Without the help, love and support of all the midwives noted here, this book never would have come to life.

I owe each and every one of you a huge standing ovation...

Murph – I hope you and Mom are looking down and smiling. Thank you for giving me your all. Like you told me, I always give them lots of teeth and think of you. Your example made me fearless!

Jared, Ariane and Vanessa – have taught me more about life than I could have ever possibly taught them. I continue to marvel at all your accomplishments. Thank you three for being my muses. You make your mom very proud!

Angie Cleary – arteest extraordinare, who can take all the crazy ideas in my head and make them look pretty on paper.

Rosmarie Epaminondas-Boehm – the most interesting woman in the world, who led by example and encouraged me for years to sit down and write. She generously edited this book, honestly told me my first title sucked and tirelessly brainstormed with me over tea until we came up with a new one.

To all the vacationing families from Vacationkids who have taught me how to be a teacher and helper for the past 15 years – I salute you. So many of your lessons are found in this book.

My fellow Vacationkids staff and agents – work ridiculously hard to help our clients enjoy fabulous vacations year after year.

Mary Lynn Sensale, RN – after living with me I don't understand how she's been a friend for the past 30 years, I simply thank God for her.

Susan Mehalko – I thank you my dear friend, aficionado, sounding board and fellow crispy French fry lover for all her encouragement, advice and hours of listening.

Brad Panik – thanks for reading my ugly first draft, being so honest and always making me laugh more than humanly possible.

Andrea Fenton – A queen among editors (or is that amongst). Either way thank you for ending my sleepless nights.

To Pat Black and the Stitch & Bitch girls – our Wednesday nights were the key to my sanity while keeping a lock on my OCD knitting while completing this project.

Lou Edwards – Thank You my captain, for sharing your expertise, helping me put all my ideas into action and making me finally realize perfection is a curse.

This book is dedicated to Brian Black

My white Knight and the champion of my dreams.

You bring out my best

I love you so much more than any words.

« Introduction »

You work hard for that cherished week of vacation with the family. When it comes time to start planning your escape, most parents immediately start thinking about juggling everyone's schedules and finding the cheapest online airfares.

Think again!

A family vacation is FAR more than just a fun week at the beach!

Sure, you need a break from the boss and housework. You want to splurge, "live a little" and have some fun. But consider this...

Childhood memories of family vacations stay with us for a lifetime. They help to shape our character and create important memories that will bind families together for generations. They evoke strong feelings of nostalgia and can be a treasured sense of comfort far into the future.

In reality, childhood is a very small window of opportunity that is given to parents. Sure, when you're changing diapers and potty training it may seem like an eternity. Turn around and your "babies" are heading off to college as you wave goodbye to parenthood in the rearview mirror.

Let's say the average family takes one week of vacation each year. Few of us can remember events prior to the age of three. This means parents have only about 15 chances to create vacation memories with our kids.

Considering these facts, family vacations should be considered precious and handled with great care.

Most parents consider a family vacation to be a luxury. They fail to appreciate the vital importance travel plays in education and the development of children. Getting the family away from daily responsibilities, routines and stress gives everyone the time to have fun, play and simply be present with one another. It also stretches our boundaries, stimulates our dreams and challenges our perceptions.

There are some parents who believe traveling with kids is simply too daunting or difficult. They will procrastinate on taking family vacations thinking the task will eventually become much easier as their children get older. They fail to appreciate that you can never make up for lost time.

Leaving one's home or comfort zone creates an element of fear for many people. Many believe the idea of a staycation means there is no need to worry about one's safety, let alone the safety of their children. Yet if we take a deeper look beyond the scare tactics of the media, we all recognize there are as many risks in our own backyards as there are out there in the big wide world. In addition, we also need to ask ourselves the question, "What type of example are we setting for our kids?" Do we embrace the world with a sense of wonder and adventure or do we prefer to simply stay locked away at home?

As a young parent, I too viewed family vacations as a time for fun. If my kids learned something new along the way, I considered it a bonus. Now with grown kids, I can look back and fully appreciate the positive impact our vacations had in changing their perspectives and enhancing their lives.

Our family travel experiences helped to mold and shape their personalities in ways I could never have imagined. As I began to write this book, I pulled out dusty photos, videos and journals. I started to reflect on how our family vacations have affected my children. Here are a few pivotal moments and the lessons learned...

Independence – CRUISE 1986 – "Go enjoy yourself Mom and don't worry, I'll play here in the club and you go have fun... We'll do lunch." (Instructions given to me by my toddler son).

Responsibility – CALIFORNIA 1987 – "I feel so sad that I forgot Aye-Aye bear on the plane. He's my best friend. I hope somebody will take care of him just like Paddington Bear."

Consequences – FLORIDA 1989 – "I never thought fire ant bites would hurt this bad. Guess I should have stopped and listened to the guy from the hotel when he yelled at me for walking on the lawn barefoot. I thought he was just being mean about the rules but he was really trying to keep me safe. Next time I'll listen better."

Empathy – WILLIAMSBURG, VIRGINIA 1990 – "We're checking in late because my sister was carsick the whole ride so we had to keep stopping. We're all tired and it's been a long day for all of us, especially my sister so she really needs a good, quiet room so she can rest and feel better."

Patience – NYC BLIZZARD OF 1993 – "Let's deal with reality, there's a snowstorm and our plane is stuck. Whining isn't going to get us anywhere so let's figure out something to keep busy, make the best of this situation and not make Mom crazy."

Tolerance – BOSTON 1994 –- "Getting stuck in traffic due to a gay rights parade while trying to see the Freedom Trail is really what freedom of speech is all about. Now I get it."

Pride – GERMANY 1995 – "The one thing that really impressed me the most? ...because I was a visitor at their school, they played the 'Star-Spangled Banner' to welcome me. It made me feel really proud to be an American."

Respect – THAILAND 1996 – "I planned to wear a different outfit today but I understand the way I dress means I show respect to the religious people at their temple. Just don't show any of these pictures to my friends please."

Cooperation – JAMAICA 1997 – "Instead of us all fighting about where we want to go today, how about we each pick one day when each of us gets to plan a day of our trip."

Courage – TURKS AND CAICOS 1999 – "When I stepped in the water and all those little fish came after my red toenail polish, it freaked me out. I was really afraid. Now I'm glad I was brave enough to go snorkeling, swimming and make friends with that big sea turtle."

Manners – MEXICO 2001 – "You know what, Mom... it really doesn't matter too much if you can't speak somebody's language.

You just have to learn to say *PLEASE, THANK YOU, HELLO and GOODBYE*, and you can pretty much smile and point to everything else. People will figure it out and want to help you."

Curiosity – LONDON 2002 – "Mom, I wonder how many windows the Queen has in Buckingham Palace? Can we stop for a minute and try to count them?"

Perseverance – HAWAII 2003 – "I swallowed so much water that I thought I was going to puke but I did it! I got up on that surfboard and rode a wave to shore. It doesn't matter that we didn't get it on video, I know I did it and that's all that matters!"

Humility – DOMINICAN REPUBLIC 2004 – "After visiting that family in their home and seeing how hard they worked on their farm growing coffee, it really makes me want to help people when I grow up."

Assertiveness – ICELAND 2005 – "I was so lost and couldn't understand any of the signs. Once I asked for help everyone was so nice. They invited me to join them for dinner and I made some new friends, so it all worked out."

Problem Solving – FRANCE 2006 – "We couldn't figure out how to get our French rental car to go into reverse. We finally found the only English-speaking person in the French countryside, and Murphy's Law, she didn't know how to drive. She waited while we flagged down a tow truck driver. He told her how to operate the car so that she could help translate his instructions into English for us. Eventually we were on our way again."

Generosity – PERU 2010 – "I'm glad we packed extra school supplies for the kids here. I also gave the teacher my souvenir money to help buy lunch for some of the kids instead of buying something stupid to bring home."

Sense of Adventure – NEW ZEALAND 2011 – "Mom, I wanted to thank you for letting me go by myself with my class to New Zealand, so I got you a souvenir – it's a photo of me bungee jumping off of their tallest bridge!" (*Important note to all parents: immediately hug your teen and say a quiet prayer of gratitude for her continued safety while you thank her for your souvenir. This thoughtful moment came from the same child* *who was forever carsick and too afraid to put her toes in seawater).*

Travel changes our attitudes. Sharing vacation adventures with our children offers so many unexpected learning opportunities. These real world experiences offer parents the opportunities to reinforce important values that are often difficult to teach. Truths that serendipitously come to us while traveling offer so many invaluable lessons. They help to create profound memories that your family will long remember.

For the past 15 years, I've dedicated myself to helping families live their travel dreams and to create vacation memories together. During this time, I've consulted with thousands of families. I've listened to all of their concerns, answered their questions and shared the joys of their experiences.

My goal in writing this book was to share my knowledge and experiences to help empower parents to become more fearless when it comes to traveling with their kids. If one child's life is changed by a vacation, then I've done my job.

If you're truly blessed in life, life will give you a few "do-overs." While writing this book, my first grandchild was born. As each word was typed, I imagined how travel and adventure will affect his life. I can't wait to start creating new vacation memories with him. I hope he inherits my wanderlust!

As much as our lives have changed since his mom was born, much has remained constant. My daughter is now just as nervous taking her little one on his first vacation as I was 30 years ago taking her on our first flight together. After a little reassurance and a bit of a pep talk, she is now ready for her first fearless family vacation.

This is the reason I created *Fearless Family Vacations*. I want to inspire, teach, empower and encourage as many parents as possible to explore and embrace the world with their kids. I believe it will make tomorrow's world a much happier place for us all.

« Chapter One »

DIFFERENT KIND OF TRAVEL BOOK

What is the BEST family vacation?

UGH! I cannot tell you how many times press people have asked me that question over the years. This same question takes many forms:

What is the best vacation for teens?

Which is the best family hotel in Hawaii?

Where can I find the best baby-friendly hotel?

My answer is always the same – there is no one single BEST of anything!

"The BEST_____ (fill in this blank) is the one that is best suited to the wishes and needs of your family." Period.

Vacations are not commodities.

Families and vacations are not "one size fits all."

The best family vacations are the ones that offer the best opportunities for your own family. When it comes to family vacations, it's all relative (pun intended). This book will help you identify all of your options, plan accordingly and help you find the BEST vacation for YOUR family.

This Is Not a Typical Family Travel Book

The purpose of this book is to help parents understand the value of family vacations and to teach parents how to properly plan to get the most vacation for their hard-earned money.

Family trips together don't have to be expensive or extravagant, but they do need to be a priority. Family vacations should be a time for everyone to have fun, renew, recharge, learn, share experiences and bond. The benefits to our children far outweigh any reasons for staying home.

Travel is an important life skill. Great family vacations are not simply created by making reservations with a few clicks of a mouse. If parents learn how to plan and travel properly, they will in turn pass these skills on to their children. Families that embrace and encourage the idea of travel find freedom, fun and experiences beyond their wildest dreams. The adventures you experience together will offer stories that will be shared around the dinner table for generations.

Most family travel books are written by travel writers. These books open us up to a world of possibilities while lighting up our imaginations. This is not that kind of travel book.

Please don't get me wrong here. Some of my best friends are travel writers. I am a HUGE fan of their work and what they do. I believe we all need a little fire put into our souls and under our behinds every now and again. An in-depth review of the top 10 family beaches in the world may be considered great travel writing by some, but it will not help your family with practical details on how to actually get out and visit these dots on the map.

There are tons of great destination guidebooks that are chock-full of details suggesting what families should see and do in every corner of the globe. This isn't that kind of travel book either.

These types of resources are like putting the cart before the horse. Sure it's fun to go zip lining in Costa Rica but shouldn't we worry about getting you all there first? It's like deciding on which curtains to hang before the house has been built. These types of books often encourage travelers to put the cart before the horse.

Again, don't get me wrong—I am a huge fan of guidebooks. Admittedly, I'm old school and like to travel with a trusty guidebook for when my smartphone craps out. When traveling overseas, it's far cheaper than paying the roaming charges! Honestly, I normally do not purchase a guidebook until after I have made my reservations. Guidebooks offer plenty of tips but first you have to get to where you're going. Also, the destination you've chosen off the bookstore shelf may or may not be the "best" fit at this stage for your family or for this particular time in your lives.

Other family travel books are written by bloggers and parents who have ventured forth with their own brood. They share firsthand experiences they learned while planning their own travels. These firsthand accounts illustrate the possibilities and, again, help to inspire other parents. Their tips and insights may have worked wonders for their family but that may not mean their experiences will help you.

Admittedly, my first job is to be a mom. I do share some of my family's personal trials and triumphs, but this book is much more. But once again, what works for my family may not be ideal for your family.

This book was written by a travel agent.

Travel agents are generally not typical travel book authors. For over 15 years, I've helped thousands of families get answers, customize itineraries, create memories and have tons of fun. It's my job to focus on the nitty-gritty and the practical side of travel. It's my job to navigate and focus on all the logistics. I sketch out the organization lines of each itinerary and then consult with my clients to help them color in all the fun experiences and memorable details.

I've done this for families of every shape, size, age and combination imaginable. It's my job to get them all from point A to point B safely, affordably and comfortably while making all of their dreams come true. This book may not be a sexy read, but I hope parents will find it helpful. I will save my funny travel anecdotes and wild tales of adventure for another volume or perhaps a future epic Hollywood movie.

Many people think travel agents have gone the way of the dinosaurs and became extinct in the age of the internet. Parents think they can now simply look online after their kids are tucked into bed, search google and voilà—vacation done. Who needs a travel agent anymore?

Today's travel agent is a decision counselor and consultant.

Anyone searching Google for "the best family vacation" will be presented with 115 million choices. More choices at our fingertips creates even more responsibility, research, confusion and frustration. Of course, we've already discussed the meaning of the word "best" when it comes to choosing a vacation.

Others think being a travel agent is glamourous. They imagine travel agents jetting off on free trips to exotic locales, nibbling gourmet hors d'oeuvres while sipping champagne from some penthouse beachfront balcony. As if!

In reality we travel agents are paying our own way to visit jungle hard hat construction zones, knee deep in rainy season mud and mosquitoes so that we can offer intelligent answers when parents want to be the first to book a room at this new resort.

I want to change the public perception on how to plan family vacations.

Parents truly want to travel with their kids. Most simply don't know how to properly plan a fun, affordable and memorable vacation with their children. Most are lost when it comes to travel planning and achieving their dreams. They need a road map, a GPS and proper advice from a trusted travel partner to make wise and efficient travel decisions while avoiding costly mistakes. I trust this book will help.

4

In my role of travel agent, I want to work with parents who are informed consumers, organized, and who understand how the travel industry works. With this understanding we can partner together to create the BEST family vacation, fully customized to the wishes and needs of you and your family, not anyone else's.

As a mom, I hate to hear stories of family vacations that have gone wrong. Not only are family vacations an investment of hard-earned money, but most importantly, BAD family vacations are an important investment of precious time that we can never get back. If you buy a cheap pair of jeans that don't fit, you can return simply return them to the store. You cannot "take back" your vacation. Most parents get less than 15 chances to take a family vacation with their children. You only have a few chances to get it right. Time is something that offers no do-overs.

For those DIY parents who still choose to Google search their travel plans, my hope is that this book will offer you a safety net and some understanding so that you can avoid many potential pitfalls and travel scams.

That is why I wrote this book. It is meant to offer sound, time-tested, practical and professional advice on planning vacations with your children no matter their age or your family's circumstances.

With a bit of professional help, some trusted techniques and affordable strategies, parents CAN give their kids the world while teaching them important life lessons that will never found in any schoolbook.

« Chapter Two »

THIS MOM'S STORY

Note – *This is indeed a nonfiction book. All of the events noted here, believe it or not, really did happen.*

You simply cannot make this stuff up!

Flashback to 1993 – Meet an unemployed, divorced mother with three young children. I had been working as a registered pediatric nurse in a busy specialty hospital for many years. In the midst of moving, motherhood and mayhem, I had let my license lapse. Renewing my nursing license would have been a long and costly venture. Survival was my immediate priority. I had no idea how I was going to make ends meet. A family vacation was a complete impossibility and the absolute farthest thing from my mind. Life as we all knew it had changed drastically. My kids were having a really difficult time coping with our new reality. I felt depressed and completely hopeless.

But wait, it gets worse...

One bright, sunny morning, my kids ran to the mailbox to find a postcard from Disney World sent from their dad. He had promised to take them there "someday" for as long as we all could remember. Instead that "someday" never came. He left, took his new girlfriend instead of his kids and wrote home about it. The look of disappointment and tears on those little faces is something I will never forget.

That night I used the balance on my last remaining credit card to book us a trip to Disney World. Beyond the impending financial doom I was creating for myself, I had even greater fears. The thought of managing three small children safely through airports and Disney World was completely overwhelming. As my kids cheerfully looked forward to our vacation, I spent many sleepless nights filled with dread, worry and panic attacks.

That vacation to Disney World transformed my family!

Even though we ended up spending a couple extra days at the airport due to a historic East Coast snowstorm, everything worked out perfectly in the end. The fighting and bickering ceased. Everyone pulled together, behaved and got along. Best of all, we smiled and laughter returned. We had fun together for the first time in many months!

Even though it took me a few of years and a whole lot of credit card interest to finally pay off this vacation, I would do it all over again in a heartbeat. This wasn't about a trip to Disney or keeping up with my ex. This vacation was all about confidence, independence, leadership, bonding and the celebration of the idea that no matter what, my family was going to be okay.

As coincidences happen, shortly after returning home from our Disney trip I landed a job working for a startup Internet travel company. Back then, most people had no idea what the Internet was, let alone what it could do. Believe it or not, at that time the only qualification I had that landed me the job was that I knew what email was and how to send one. This was a skill I learned from my son's librarian as a tactic to keep him interested at school.

That internet startup consisted of five people working out of a barn, with no heat or indoor plumbing. We had to walk down the lane to a nearby farmhouse to use the bathroom. I spent winter days wrapped in coats and sleeping bags to keep warm. Our resident geek worked with us virtually from Utah via a dial-up Internet connection.

It was a very exciting time with incredible opportunities. Every minute that I wasn't hard at work, I was inspired to learn everything there was to know about the travel industry. Soon I was running all the publicity and marketing for our company.

One morning I was summoned into the boss's office. I was convinced I had created some major catastrophe by breaking the Internet or something of equal devastation. He explained that he had been invited to speak at a travel conference in London. Due to family obligations he could not attend and had decided to send me as his representative.

With less than a week's notice I would be taking my first international trip—alone! In addition to making travel arrangements, I had to make childcare arrangements, get a passport, write a speech, present that speech in front of industry leaders, figure out what to wear and find time to buy a suitcase!

With absolutely no time to think, I flew to London on my first international adventure all by my big self. As my taxi first drove past Big Ben I was so overwhelmed that I cried. Never in a million years had I ever expected to find myself in London... and that was just the beginning of many wild adventures!

Being a novice traveler, I neglected to notify my credit card company that I'd be traveling abroad (something I had never done before). Imagine how shocked I was to arrive at hotel check-in that fateful Saturday morning, thousands of miles away from home, only to find that my credit and debit cards had been put on hold due to suspected fraudulent activity. I found myself penniless in London until Monday morning. It was thanks to the generosity of the hotel manager that I had something to eat that weekend and cab fare to my important Monday morning meeting.

Thankfully, despite all the stress, my business meeting and speaking engagement were a huge success. My credit card woes were sorted, and I treated the hotel manager to a "posh" dinner Monday evening to thank him for his kindness and understanding.

Soon I found myself being invited to speak and attend meetings all over the planet—from Amsterdam to Kuala Lumpur, from Toronto to Singapore, from Paris to San Diego. I was given even more responsibilities, including vacation product development, airline contracts and developing the very first forum to handle online travel reviews.

As my travel experience grew so did my attitudes, opinions and insights. The world became a much smaller and increasingly fascinating place. Teaching my kids and sharing these experiences became a huge priority. The quantity of time I had to share as a traveling single working mom was limited. I wanted to ensure that the quality of time I spent with my kids was of the highest caliber.

Thanks to my many years spent as a road warrior, I quickly learned every trick in the book to make travel easier and more affordable. This knowledge enabled me to bring my kids along on many of my world adventures. Soon my children were enjoying experiences I would have never dreamed possible. Through my travel contacts, my son spent six weeks in Germany, Austria and Switzerland on a student exchange. One spring my middle daughter and I shopped our way through England, France and Belgium. Sir Richard Branson even invited my youngest daughter to dinner in London. They swapped funny stories about how their dyslexia is something that makes them both so very unique.

Naturally, as our passports acquired more and more stamps, everyone would ask me for travel tips and vacation advice. It quickly became obvious that parents yearned to travel with children but were faced with so many overwhelming questions, challenges and unique situations. To complicate matters, the travel needs of every family evolves and grows with each new child and changes with every passing year. I brought my concerns about the needs of the family travel market to my board of directors. My hope was that they would create website tools that would help busy families make the most of their vacation. My ideas fell on deaf ears.

My very own family was also evolving around this same time. In early 1998 I met the most amazing man in the world. He lived right down the road from us but it took the Internet to bring us together. Admittedly, it took a while for me to trust and open my heart up to love again, but every day since, I thank the heavens that he came into my life. We were married in the fall of 1999 and have lived and traveled happily ever since.

As the century changed, so did the dot com world. Our little company with no heat or plumbing was sold to a huge travel company for more than fifty million dollars. Instead of a good payout in recognition of my years of dedication, I was fired. This time around, unemployment wasn't so scary. When word got out that I was available, the job offers poured in. I had my pick of several wonderful opportunities. Every one of these opportunities required very long hours, even longer commutes and extensive traveling.

By now my children were teens and I knew they would soon be off on their own to college. I wanted to spend time with my new husband and build a life with him instead of facing a life on the road. In addition, my father, whose guidance, help and support had gotten me through some of my darkest times was now ailing and in need of my help. My family was my priority yet I wanted to continue to work in a career that I loved.

In 2001, with the support of my family, the need to help other parents travel with their kids and an "HTML for Dummies" book, the Vacationkids.com family travel website was born. The idea was to create a travel agency that specifically catered to the travel needs of families with kids, offering the expert help, guidance and advice parents would appreciate.

To my surprise and chagrin, even after all my worldwide travel experience and sales, I didn't qualify for a travel agency license. Understanding where the online travel industry was headed and thanks to the pressure and persistence of many of my peers, the rules were changed. Vacationkids was granted one of the first online travel agency licenses.

Vacationkids officially launched August 1, 2001, to rave reviews. My staff and I were overwhelmed with initial inquiries and a huge number of reservations. During that first month, Disney World was offering an amazing "Kids Stay, Play and Fly Free" deal. We made a huge number of reservations in record time. All my hard work was paying off. Vacationkids was now a reality and we were proud to offer parents the information and help they needed to get out and explore the world with their children.

One month later... 9/11!

The entire nation mourned in a complete state of shock. Our hearts broke for all who died and especially for all those left behind to grieve and wonder. Planes were grounded for nearly two weeks. Fear crept into all our hearts.

This was probably the absolute worst time in all of history to open a travel agency/website. As I stared at the devastating television news scenes praying for all those touched by this event, I also thought my dreams for Vacationkids were over. I figured I would soon be dusting off my resume and making yet another career change.

Then a very surprising thing happened—nobody cancelled!

Disney World evacuated their parks on the day of the attacks. It opened the very next day despite a tropical storm in Florida and national travel warnings. As we notified our clients of their options, we were honestly surprised that none of our clients wanted to cancel their reservations.

Despite their obvious fears and concerns, spending quality time with the people they loved the most in this world became their highest priority. The thought of cancelling their vacation plans meant that the terrorists would have succeeded with their evil plans to defeat our spirit and freedom. Those who were thwarted by grounded flights simply applied for reimbursement from the airlines and packed their cars for a road trip. Those stranded in the park by grounded flights resumed their daily schedules and endured long lines waiting for answers and a means to get back home. To this day I remember speaking with our returning families. Just about everyone reported how their hearts were touched by members of the Disney cast and music bands in the park rallying concerned guests by leading everyone in patriotic songs.

Since that humble beginning, Vacationkids has grown and thrived thanks to the support of our clients and their referrals. Although it makes us feel a bit "old," we're proud to now be arranging destination weddings, travel events and even corporate meetings for many of our original vacation "kids" who are now all grown up and starting families of their own.

Over the years, we've learned a thing or two about how to help families get the best value and most incredible experiences out of their vacation. As travel trends and the needs of our clients have changed, we too have evolved and found new solutions and alternatives. It is the reason for this book and the reason we look forward to heading to our office each and every day.

So Why Bother Sharing My Story?

I never dreamed I would ever be able to afford or visit all of the amazing places I've seen, let alone share these memories with my children. I consider myself very blessed that despite drama and trauma, I was able to give the gift of travel to my kids.

I know every parent wants to give their kids the world. Parents naturally want their children to have every opportunity to thrive and succeed. Perhaps many think they do not have the means, knowledge or even insight to obtain these dreams for their children. I hope that by sharing my story, industry knowledge and secrets I can help other families achieve their travel dreams too.

I was raised in a home where a family vacation meant a road trip to Grandma's house or sharing a cottage on Cape Cod for a week. Vacations were never a priority when my kids were first born.

With our budget (or should I say lack of budget), vacations felt impossible. Once I began to realize the important and positive influence travel had on my children, vacation time became a priority. With understanding and clear goals it's amazing how the "impossible" can quickly become a reality.

I hope that by sharing my knowledge here, many other families will be able to experience the wonder, insight, education and the many other gifts that travel offers. By inspiring our children to become citizens of the world, perhaps we can make our collective futures brighter.

« Chapter Three »

SIX STEPS FOR PLANNING THE PERFECT FAMILY VACATION

Picture This Scenario:

It's been a very long and highly stressful day at work. You're late picking up the kids from band practice and ballet. Your breakfast consisted of a power bar and coffee. Lunch never materialized so now you're starving. The fridge is empty so you stop by your local market to grab something quick for dinner. You realize, as you unpack your bags of groceries, you bought a whole lot of junk food but neglected to buy the proper ingredients you needed to cook dinner... So you call for pizza delivery. As you hang up the phone, your spouse walks in complaining that they had pizza for lunch that day while your kids explain that they had snacks after school and aren't hungry.

Sound familiar?

If you're smiling and shaking your head in agreement then congratulations and welcome to the club. I would also venture to guess that this scene has happened more than once in your household. For most families, this is "normal."

So what do you think happens when most "normal" families try to plan a vacation?

Sometime around the middle of May, Mom sends a text saying, "We need a vacation." Dad replies, "Go ahead and plan something for June." Mom spends the next few weeks eating yogurt on her break so she can hunt online for vacation ideas and travel deals. She's confused and overwhelmed by all the options and choices. She finally finds their ideal vacation and excitedly shares it with her family. Dad then informs her that she picked the exact dates for his regional meeting so that won't work for him, while their daughter thinks her choice of hotel is lame. Determined, she goes back online with her new search criteria but now finds prices have taken a huge jump. She's completely frustrated. As a last-ditch effort, she calls a travel agent and says, "We're looking to go on vacation in two weeks. We want to go someplace warm and cheap."

In both of these situations there are obvious problems with priorities, communication and proper planning. Pizza leftovers can be frozen and reheated. A poorly planned vacation experience is costly both financially and emotionally. There are no do-overs or leftovers here.

These parents are stressed, overworked and tired. They simply view a vacation as a break from the rat race. If they fully understood how much impact a family vacation has on the future success of their children, as well as the emotional health of their family, this entire scenario would be much different.

Perhaps your family is ready to make travel a priority? ...How do you get started and where do you even begin?

"Planning a quality family vacation is just like planning a family... you need to start working at least nine months in advance."

Most parents will smile, relate and hopefully remember the "nine months" timeline here. It's an easy way to remember an important fact about how the travel industry works. Travel products get more expensive the closer you get to your departure date.

Most airlines publish their rates and schedules about 300–330 days in advance. Cruise lines and many resorts publish their rates about 500 days in advance. If you must travel during December holidays or spring break weeks, you may have to book your accommodations and then add flights as soon as they are available. Booking the main components of your vacation at least nine months in advance will afford you the best selection when it comes to schedule, room availability and even prices. Advanced planning will also help you to save and budget wisely while avoiding last-minute price spikes.

Often, parents will argue that they cannot possibly plan their life that far ahead in advance. Work, school, sports and activity schedules simply will not permit that type of advance commitment. These are the folks that have yet to embrace the idea of vacations being an important investment in their child's future. A vacation has not yet become a priority for their family.

These same parents will argue that they plan to take advantage of fantastic "last-minute deals." They have read online that if you wait until 60 days prior to departure and book your trip at precisely 3:05 p.m. on the second Tuesday of the month during the full moon of a lunar eclipse they will ultimately win the cheap travel lottery. In return, I will ask these same parents, "When was the last time you saw a pink unicorn playing in your backyard?"

A last-minute family vacation deal is just about as mythical as that pink unicorn. All the smart families will have planned ahead and booked all the best spots. Sure you may see some TV news travel "expert" boasting about some wonderful Caribbean resort being offered at 40% off during the December holidays. If you see it on TV, it must be true—right? That "expert" neglected to mention that there are only two rooms left at this price and that the last-minute airfare for your family will cost well over $10,000 to get there... so if you and the kids can swim several hundred miles, it's a fabulous deal!

For parents who are afraid to commit to advance vacation planning for fear of paying more, please know many travel companies will honor any last-minute sales that may result in a price less than what you originally paid. For those companies that don't, you can usually purchase travel insurance to cover the difference—something necessary for most families anyway.

If you truly want your family's vacation to meet or better yet, exceed your expectations for fun, learning and adventure, then you have to be willing to invest the commitment of time to properly plan your trip. Truly great vacation experiences don't magically happen. They need to be well-planned, designed and customized.

There is an entire world of fun, exciting and fascinating family vacations to choose from. Most families are limited to only one or two weeks of vacation time per year. Many families may only be able to afford a vacation every other year or every three years. Most children are with their parents for 18 short years prior to their departure for college. Chances are your children won't remember much before their fourth birthday. When you crunch these numbers into perspective, it is obvious that we only have a few opportunities to get vacations right, especially if you want to make lasting impressions that will impact the future of your kids.

Every new journey begins with a map and the same holds true for vacation planning. Having some structural guidelines in place for vacation planning will make the process far easier. It's like heading to the grocery store with an organized shopping list and a full belly. It will save you hours of fruitless searching and frustration. The reward will be the family vacation of your dreams.

Having a vacation planning guide will also help you to focus and find the absolute best vacations that match your family's dreams, needs and lifestyle. It will allow you to make quick and informed decisions which are skills necessary for scoring the best travel deals. Ultimately it will help you to create fantastic experiences that will have the most impact on your child's future.

Vacation planning ultimately boils down to answering six guideline questions. It starts by answering important travel planning questions that will influence all of the travel decisions that you make. Each time you consider and answer one of these questions, your family is one step closer to the perfect vacation.

Each of these six questions acts like a piece to a jigsaw puzzle. Every answer of this travel-planning puzzle affects the other pieces. When all of the questions are answered, all the pieces come together and you can finally see the big picture of what your family vacation will be. This system creates a beautiful picture almost by magic. If just one of the questions is left blank or not answered properly, it's like missing a piece of the puzzle. The entire picture changes, something is lacking and the outcome for all of your effort is far less than satisfactory.

Parents should start discussing these six questions at least one year in advance. Answering these questions requires time to think and honest, face-to-face communication with everyone in the family.

The other point to bear in mind here is that answering these six questions is not a once-and-done activity. These same questions will necessitate new and different answers each and every year parents start to plan their family vacation. The reason for this is that children grow. Family situations and relationships evolve and change over the years. This will be discussed in later chapters but for now, simply understand that these six guideline questions are, for years to come, the basic foundation for all travel planning you will do.

Parents need to include the children in their vacation planning conversations based on their age, maturity and level of understanding. Obviously if you are parents to a new infant this step is not necessary, but even young toddlers can be brought into the discussions. Parents can use tools like travel storybooks, artwork and a countdown calendar. Travel planning can be a great way to bring families together. It gives everyone something exciting to talk about and an adventure to anticipate.

Each family will need to decide for themselves how much influence the kids will be allowed in the decision-making process. If done properly, trip planning can be a very empowering learning experience for kids. If your family will be traveling to a brand new destination, the entire experience will be new for everyone. It is often the one unique situation that puts parents and children on an even playing field. Nobody is an expert or knows exactly what to expect. It requires everyone to trust one another and work together to ensure everyone's fun and happiness. A three-year-old may be given the choice to visit either the beach or the zoo. An eight-year-old can be given a souvenir money in advance and learn to set priorities and a budget for their own incidental spending. A teen might be entrusted to go online to search, budget and plan a day's worth of sightseeing activities for the entire family. Empowering your children at every age will yield greater involvement and cooperation.

Although it is very necessary to answer all of these guideline questions honestly, this is not like taking your SATs. There are no wrong answers. There are no rules carved in stone or judgments to be made. The correct answers are honest answers that make the most sense for family's individual travel needs, situation and desires.

At the end of this chapter, you'll find a worksheet with a list of these six important travel questions and space for your answers. Copy it and use it as a planning worksheet for years to come. Print out a new copy and answer these questions each and every time your family decides to leave home. Answers to each of these questions will change with every trip and every passing year.

In the meantime, let's look at the reasons behind each of these questions and why each is so very important in your search to find your perfect family vacation.

1. WHO WILL BE GOING ON VACATION?

This seems like a simple enough question, but it can create major problems for many families. Will just your immediate family be going, or will grandparents be joining you? Will all your kids be coming along, or does your youngest child prefer to stay home and visit your ex? These issues need to be discussed and decided before you start making any travel plans. Knowing who will be going will affect all other decisions like destination, accommodation, sleeping arrangements, activities and even budget.

All travelers, adults and children, should be listed. With kids, it is also very important to include their exact ages <u>at the time they will be traveling</u>. If your child is 20 months old right now but your family won't be traveling until after his second birthday, this will affect your airline ticket decisions. If your child is nine now but will be celebrating her 10th birthday at Disney World, you'll be paying more for park admission. If your child is 12 now but will be 13 by the time spring break rolls around, it will affect your hotel rates and decisions. If Grandma is 64 now and traveling with you, she could be in for a substantial discount if she's a year older by the time the vacation rolls around. In order to obtain accurate vacation quotes and rates, it is crucial to consider everyone's age at the time they will be traveling. The number of travelers and their ages will affect other decisions, especially your budget.

Certainly there is the temptation to "fib" here if it will save a buck on your child's ticket. First of all, I would urge parents to consider what type of example they are setting for their children by promoting this sort of behavior. Secondly, consider the embarrassment you may be subjected to if you were called out in public to produce proof of age for your child. If you are sailing on a cruise or traveling overseas, birth certificates and passports will be required and checked. If someone can prove that there was any misrepresentation of the facts, it could mean cancellation of your reservations at worst, or the need to pay new, higher last-minute fares and/or penalties. Ethical travel agents would not risk their professional reputations in order to save you a couple of bucks. Parents making their own DIY reservations need to be aware of the risk they are taking.

There are important legal responsibilities for every passenger, at every age. If you are flying domestically within the United States, all adult passengers must show a photo driver's license or government-issued ID. The name on your airline tickets must match the name on your photo ID exactly. Any passenger who is flying to a foreign country, regardless of their age, must have a valid US passport, and the names used on their airline ticket

20

reservations and their dates of birth must match their passports exactly.

With cruise ships, passports are highly recommended for all passengers. If your ship sails from a US port and returns to that exact same port, passengers are allowed to use their "original" birth certificates. Birth certificates must be original documents with a raised seal. Photocopied birth certificates are not accepted. In addition, adult passengers must also present a valid photo driver's license or government-issued photo ID. Children under 16 using their original birth certificates for a cruise do not need a photo ID.

It is extremely important that the names, birth dates and genders used on all airline ticket and cruise reservations match their official forms of identification EXACTLY. Any mistakes, misspellings or omissions will mean additional hassles and may result in penalty fees. It is the responsibility of all passengers to have the proper IDs on them, ready to present at the time of departure. If you fail to do this or neglect this important responsibility, your family could be "denied boarding." This means you will not be allowed onto your airplane or cruise ship. "Denied boarding" also means you forfeit the entire cost of your vacation and this is not something covered by any travel insurance.

When families start their vacation plans and decide WHO will be traveling, this is the time to ensure a very important step. Now is the time to pull important documents like passports and birth certificates out of their "safe-keeping" spots and to review them. Use them to fill out your worksheets. Double-check and make sure you have spelled everyone's name correctly and determine whether or not full middle names or initials were used on passports. Make sure to double-check the expiration dates on everyone's passports. Nothing can ruin a long anticipated vacation more than arriving at the airport to discover one person's passport has expired.

If this will be your family's first trip overseas, you can go ahead and make your vacation reservations before you actually have your passports. Just be sure that the names, dates and genders used on your reservations exactly match all of the personal information used on your passport applications. Also be sure to allow enough time for the passport application process. Generally it takes six to eight weeks for the government to process and return new passports. This process can be expedited for last-minute or emergency travel but this is much more expensive. Remember every passenger will need to take passport photos and present documents proving their US citizenship as part of the application process along with the application fees, which are generally around $100 per person.

Full information can be found at:
http://travel.state.gov/content/travel/english.html

If you are a single parent, blended family or traveling with someone else's child, parental permission may be required. This is discussed in more detail in later chapters.

Knowing exactly who will be going will also help you select the "right" type of vacation. Will you need a resort with baby care, a teen program or does your family need both? If Grandma has mobility issues, perhaps a smaller resort with elevators will no doubt be preferable to sightseeing the jungle. Remember there is no single "best" family resort, hotel or cruise. When considering WHO is going, finding the "best" also means finding the best balance so that everyone is happy. What is "best" for one person in the family may not be "best" for the rest. The best resort for a family with a toddler would most likely be a nightmare for the family with a 15-year-old. If your family craves action on this trip, and the "Number One Best" hotel published in some travel magazine is a five-star resort in the jungle, then it is certainly not the best choice for you despite all their awards and rave reviews. The word "best" can be so very enticing and relative.

Another part of this WHO question also needs to be, "Who will be sleeping with whom?" It's not that your travel agent is trying to get all up in your business. We're just trying to make everyone happy and this means that delicate questions may need to be asked.

There are occupancy rules determining how many adults or kids are allowed to share the same hotel room or cruise cabin. Even though you may want to share the same room with your four small children, the hotel rules may not allow it. Do the parents want an upgraded suite with a master bedroom with a privacy door so that Mom and Dad can enjoy a little "romance" (AKA sex) while they are on vacation without fear of the kids watching them? Does a couple want a king bed or do they want separate beds for perhaps health reasons? Sleeping arrangements can certainly affect many other aspects of the vacation planning process.

Maybe your family will be taking separate vacations. This may be due to differing ideas of fun, budget restrictions or simply to avoid sibling bickering. Remember there is no written or absolute rule carved in stone anywhere that says everyone in the family must take the same vacation at the same time. Depending upon your family's unique circumstances or situation, separate vacations might be the right decision. In the long-term, they often work to actually bring everyone closer. Once again, this idea needs to be discussed and decided in advance during the vacation planning stages so that everyone is on the same page.

If you plan to travel with extended family and friends, the question of WHO will multiply. This will determine whether you qualify for any group discounts and specifically which type of group travel discounts will benefit your family the most. More of these details will be discussed in the chapter on multi-generational vacations and reunions.

The last (and certainly one of the most important points) to consider is the wellness and health of every person listed on your "who's who" travel list. Volumes could be written here to address each and every possible illness or ailment that could affect your family's vacation. Yet for everyone in the family to have an enjoyable, stress-free vacation, the health and special needs of every traveler must be addressed in the planning stage. In addition, the needs of caregivers deserve special attention as well.

Talk openly with your travel agent and they should be able to offer help or find resources for you. As a former pediatric nurse, I do have a slightly a deeper understanding of the needs many of my clients. That being said, there are travel agencies that specialize in accessible travel for guests with disabilities.

The more you are willing to share and the more open you are, the better your travel agent will be able to serve you. Be honest and realistic with your requirements. It is much better to be prepared and ready than being stuck, stranded and disappointed.

Maybe your child has been diagnosed with an autistic spectrum disorder and is stressed by crowds or has sensory issues with sand. Perhaps a family member has mobility issues and will need specialized equipment, assistance with boarding an aircraft, or a hotel with larger elevators (which can be a challenge in certain destinations). Even kids with allergies or asthma will need additional planning to help ensure that these challenges don't spoil their fun.

If a family member suffers from a chronic health problem, or receives routine medical care, be sure they get the green light to go on vacation from their doctor. This should be done before making any vacation deposits and confirming your reservations.

An accurate list of WHO, together with everyone's official legal names and dates of birth (M/D/Y), is a great starting point. Now that you have double checked your IDs, are aware of your legal obligations, and have double checked all passport expiry dates, you can confidently move on to more considerations.

TRAVEL PERSONALITIES

When we talk about "who" will be going on vacation, we must also appreciate that everyone has a distinct travel personality. Generally there are six different personality travel traits. Once again there is a very good chance that your family may have a few different types of travelers within its ranks. To narrow down your focus on the hunt for your perfect vacation, it is also a very good idea to consider which type of vacation will be best suited to the travel personalities in your family.

The Born Explorers – These people live to travel! They are extreme-experience seekers and adrenaline junkies. They are the type who want to visit all seven continents and have very long bucket lists. They collect destinations like trophies and keep a copy of "1,000 places to visit before you die" next to their beds. If two born explorers meet, it's best to stand back as there will be conversation dueling, and a "can you top this... ?" dialog that will begin to sound like a script from an *Indiana Jones* movie. Kid explorers will have a long list of places they want to visit. These folks embrace spontaneity while traveling because to them travel is all about the journey and discovering new things. They will seek out the less-traveled road, sleep under the stars and eat very strange foods just because they can and it's out there.

The Travel Snobs – These folks are not really divas, they just enjoy the finer things in life. It's all about great expectations and their vacation living up to them. Most are experienced travelers with a means of comparison. While they enjoy the idea of travel they just don't like being inconvenienced or leaving the comforts of home. They enjoy traveling to foreign destinations, but they appreciate being surrounded by fine amenities. When visiting a destination they will want to see major historic sites, museums and the "must sees" of that particular place. They also appreciate good insider's tips and partaking in the best experiences money can buy (especially when you can get it at a discount). Travel snobs can easily navigate public transport in foreign countries but prefer to hire a driver. They tend to have more controlling or type A personalities. There can be a bit of a disconnect when a travel snob's expectation exceeds what they can afford; that's why occasional reality checks are necessary to keep everyone on the right page.

The Typical Tourist – This is the vast majority of vacationers out there who are looking for great value for their vacation dollars and the chance to build fun and exciting memories. Tourists are easygoing folks looking for fun in all the right places. They are mostly influenced by their friends and the latest travel ads. If they visit Hawaii, they are happy to visit one island and return with hula skirt and a box of pineapples. To a tourist, this means they have "done" Hawaii. They've seen the highlights and now they are done. These are the same folks who may be a bit reluctant at first to visit Mexico, but return wearing the huge purple sombreros to board their flight home. Tourists tend to like cruises, all-inclusive resorts and theme parks. If they really love a particular destination they will return every few years but will probably want to stay at a different resort. They "say" they want new travel experiences but chances are they would be secretly happy to engage in the same type of activities year after year.

The Repeaters – These people live by the mantra "if it's not broken, don't fix it." Repeaters prefer to take the exact same vacation, generally during the same week, year after year. This may partially be a matter of family tradition, but generally these people are not big on taking risks. They hate surprises and find comfort in the same old things. They are loyal if not downright stubborn. They will be the first to say they don't like something, even if they have never tried it. Generally they prefer road trips and tend to vacation not too very far from home. They do not fly and most do not have passports. These are the families who take their first child to Disney World in a stroller and return every year even after all their kids have graduated college and left the nest. Repeaters tend to travel in packs or groups because they sense a certain safety in numbers.

The Homebodies – As the name implies, some people like to stay at home. They don't like to travel and do not find any joy making vacation plans. They are travel pessimists and can give you a long list of reasons why travel is a bad deal. Their idea of a perfect vacation is a staycation in the backyard. Often they suffer from fears or phobias that prevent them from leaving home. The only way they will go on vacation is with very strong encouragement like, for example, an important family wedding. At best they can be decent travel companions as long as they do not need to think about either planning or the itinerary. Thinking about leaving home will consume them with stress. These folks find comfort in groups. They do best on group-escorted tours where there is a tour leader to hold their hand every step of the way.

Now stop and think about the family members of your own household. Perhaps you are a typical tourist and your spouse is a homebody. Maybe your teen is an avid adventurer and you are a repeater at best. Maybe you and your spouse are both explorers but now you have a new baby in tow. It is easy to understand how different travel personalities can quickly complicate a family vacation.

Success is found in compromise and communication. Trying to force someone into being a different type of traveler will only lead to arguments, frustrations and unhappy vacations for everyone.

The good news is that just about every destination offers the opportunity to build custom itineraries that will suit any traveler's personality profile, including families with blended personalities. Often a good travel agent will spot these traits in your family and make appropriate suggestions.

Having frank conversation in advance will help avoid many conflicts that could ultimately spoil your vacation. For example, if Mom is a homebody and Dad and the kids are born explorers but it is agreed that everyone wants to visit the Caribbean, perhaps a cruise vacation would be the best choice. There's a good chance they can drive to port. Ships offer plenty of ports to explore while Mom only has to unpack once. Dad and the kids can enjoy port adventures like zip lining and snorkeling while Mom can choose to stay aboard ship.

If your family's travel personalities clash with no room for compromise, then you may want to consider separate family vacations. Surprisingly, separate vacations can often lead to more harmony and family togetherness and can make sure that even the most reluctant traveler will have a wonderful time.

Remember: there is no such thing as a "best" family vacation. The best family vacations are the ones that offer the best opportunities for the particular needs of your family.

2. WHEN WILL YOU BE GOING?

It has been said that "timing is everything." This is certainly true for vacation planning. It's not just a matter of "when" but also how much time it will take to do everything you want or need to accomplish.

Most families take their family vacations according to their school calendars. When the kids are off from school, families go on vacation. This means the most popular times for family travel are December holidays, spring break and summer vacation. Depending on your particular school district, windows of vacation opportunity may also include Thanksgiving, teacher in-service breaks or President's Day.

If this sounds like your family, BE SURE to check ahead and get the right dates from your school calendar BEFORE you start planning your vacation. This will allow you to work more efficiently, avoid frustration and prevent penalty fees for changing your reservations. If your home is in an area that can be affected by snow days, take this into consideration if you're planning your vacation for early June.

If your family has some flexibility or "wiggle room" with your travel dates, this can often impact your budget, especially if your family must travel during peak travel times. Taking a day or two off from school and either leaving a couple days early or returning a few days later can save you hundreds.

Surprisingly, it's often cheaper to stay longer. The majority of families take a seven night vacation during school breaks. Sometimes, flights are cheaper with eight, nine, or ten-night schedules and the cost difference can make up for what it would cost to stay longer in your hotel.

Travel industry sales for hotels, cruises and airline tickets are all based on supply and demand. When demand is high, prices increase. When demand is low, everything goes on sale. The same holds true for specific destinations. During the winter months of frigid temperatures and snowstorms, the demand for sunny, tropical beach vacations increases along with the price tags. Remember that many popular destinations will draw guests from around the globe. The school calendars of children from other countries may also affect pricing of particular travel dates.

Travel demand also increases the closer you get to departure. This is due to all the folks looking for that last-minute, pink unicorn. Many desperate travelers will simply fold and pay the higher price. Others will find it beyond their means. Still, limited space and more demand yield higher prices.

Bearing these principles in mind will help you choose your vacation weeks a bit more wisely. December holiday hotel and cruise rates are released about one year in advance and sell out quickly. Often, hotel and cruise space will need to be booked even before flight schedules and flight rates are available to avoid sellouts.

Spring break and even summer vacation plans need to start during the previous summer months. For the best availability and prices, reservations should be made as soon as the school calendars for the upcoming year have been published. Once again, whenever possible, start vacation planning at least NINE months in advance.

However, if your children are not yet of school age, if you homeschool or live in a school district open to other learning opportunities, try to plan your vacation during a time when your budget will go a bit farther. Late August, September and the weeks between Thanksgiving and the December holidays usually offer the lowest rates. There may also be a window of opportunity between Easter and the summer vacation, depending on how the dates fall each year. It may be difficult to take the kids out of school for an entire week, but perhaps you can schedule one or two days off after a long weekend and still get away.

There is also the great debate amongst parents as to whether or not to take kids out of school for family vacations. This is a decision that each parent will need to make for their own children. Of course, some children are far more academic. A few days out of school would not harm their grades. Other students may struggle with one or more subjects and fall behind if they were to miss school. Your family may have children who fall into both categories. Before you make the decision to take your child out of school, be sure to check with the specific rules set forth by your local school or district. Speak to teachers and school administrators and make sure you are making the right decisions about school before you begin planning your trip.

Many novice travelers are concerned about making vacation plans during "hurricane season." For the Caribbean and Mexico, hurricane season generally runs from early June until the end of October. Of course this coincides with most school summer vacations. Apart from the increased threat of severe tropical storms, this is also the rainy or wet season for most tropical locations.

In reality, this means it usually rains every day but it's normally for just a few minutes. It's not an all-day deluge. It is the reason why these areas draw us to visit with their lush beauty and gorgeous tropical flowers. Within 15 minutes, the sun is again out and everything is dry, as if the rain never happened. This is also why the seven-day weather forecasts for most Caribbean destinations during the summer months will show rain every day of the week. It certainly does not mean your vacation will be a washout.

Bear in mind that the "Caribbean" is a HUGE geographical area. A storm in one part may not impact other locations. It would be like saying one shouldn't travel to New York because of wildfires in California.

If concerns over the weather are keeping you from exploring the world with your kids, remember no matter where you are, weather happens. A couple years ago a friend scolded me for traveling to Mexico during hurricane season. We had perfect weather during our week in Mexico. We returned home to Pennsylvania the day before Hurricane Sandy devastated the East Coast of the United States and found ourselves without power for several days. You just never know!

There is travel insurance protection that allows you to "cancel for any reason." If prior to your departure there is a weather issue of

Sally Black

any kind—hurricane or snowstorm—you can simply cancel your trip for a full refund.

If you want your family to enjoy certain specific experiences during your travels together, then you will often have to time your trip accordingly. If your dream is to visit Amsterdam to see the tulips of the Keukenhof Gardens, you have to know that this event only happens in early spring. Alaska offers its most popular tours and cruises during the summer. Want to see baby sea turtles hatching, then you need to plan your vacation during the fall and preferably during a full moon (no, not kidding about the moon this time). If seeing a humpback whale breaching in the open ocean is something you want to share with your children, then you need to plan your Pacific Coast vacation during the winter months. Certain natural phenomena only occur during specific times of the year. For these life experiences you will need to plan your family's journey using Mother Nature's clock.

Timing not only involves your departure and return dates, it also plays a huge role in daily itineraries. Some families insist on jam-packed daily schedules similar to military maneuvers. Others fail to plan and simply prefer to go with the flow. When it comes to daily schedules there needs to be a happy balance. Priorities should be scheduled with an appropriate amount of time to keep the pace of your vacation relaxed. Often the most wonderful memories from any family vacation are the unexpected ones that occur serendipitously. If you focus too much on a schedule, you may miss the chance to stop and smell the beautiful roses.

3. WHAT TYPE OF VACATION DOES YOUR FAMILY WANT?

Is your family looking for a relaxed vacation, free from alarm clocks and deadlines? Are you looking for an adrenaline rush of non-stop adventure? Would you prefer to immerse yourself in the culture and feel like a local? Do you want to drive, fly, sail,

31

hike or climb to your destination? Does your family need free WiFi or want to be completely unplugged? One destination or vacation can offer many different itinerary choices or vacation styles.

More often than not, your family will be a combo platter of all of these travel personalities noted earlier. It will take open communication and cooperation to find a destination, accommodation and daily itineraries balanced to suit everyone. The travel personalities of your family members will help in selecting the style of your family's vacation. In turn, this will also influence your budget.

Some travelers are perfectly fine with a hotel that is "clean and comfortable." Others may require luxury, location and fine amenities. If Mom expects to be pampered on vacation and Dad chooses a hotel that does not offer a spa or room service, there may be fireworks, and not the good kind! A born adventurer may prefer to head off the beaten path while a tourist would prefer to be near area attractions.

What type of vacation you choose will certainly influence the amount of your travel budget. Everyone wants to get the most value for their hard-earned vacation dollars. This also means reality checks and proper expectations. Just about every family-friendly destination will offer budget, moderate and luxury accommodations.

Some families may have different sleep patterns that may impact your choices. Parents of young infants (perhaps wakeful throughout the night) may want to have child care during the day so that they can rest or catch up on some sleep. Mom and Dad may be early risers heading off to the gym at dawn and relaxing with a glass of wine in the evening. Their teens may prefer to sleep until noon so that they can meet and chat with their peers until the wee hours of the morning. If Grandpa snores, perhaps for the sanity of everyone, he should have his own room. These body rhythms and preferences must be taken into account as you plan your itinerary.

Your family may enjoy specific activities together, for example, skiing, horseback riding, or perhaps scuba diving. Obviously your choice of destination and accommodation would need to offer these options. Remember a travel itinerary can be built around any specific interest your family may enjoy—baseball, shopping, dinosaurs, food, history, music or whatever. If you're really clever, you can roll all of these items on your wish list into one fun itinerary. Consider a long weekend in New York City. You can see a baseball game, go shopping, visit the dinosaurs at the Natural History Museum, include a boat ride to Ellis Island to discover your family's roots, and even order a gourmet picnic to take to a free concert in Central Park for a night of music under the stars.

If your family is heading for a destination that offers a great deal of sightseeing, this question becomes very important. Let's say your family wants to visit Italy. Do you prefer a guided tour that moves hotels every night so that you can cover a great deal of territory in a short amount of time? Do you appreciate the hand-holding of a tour guide and being in the company of other travelers? Do you prefer not to be tied to a tour schedule and would you prefer to remain independent travelers? Does your family have enough travel experience to find your way around and see everything on your wish list? Can you navigate public transport in a foreign country or do you need a private guide? If you prefer not to keep changing hotels each night, can you accomplish your sightseeing goals without long commutes? Would a cruise give you the option of independent travel with daily excursions while avoiding packing and unpacking every night? Which option is the best fit for your family? Can you see how the same destination can be visited a number of different ways depending on the "style," or what kind of trip will best suit the needs of your family?

There are many different ways to create the perfect itinerary and style to meet the travel needs of your family. Having clearly set goals and guidelines for your vacation expectations will most certainly help. It will allow you to focus on making the right choices and help you to find that "best" vacation that is perfect for your family.

4. WHERE DO YOU WANT TO GO?

Often the difficult part when it comes to selecting a vacation spot is not choosing a place to go but rather finding the exact spot to place that pin on the map. It usually comes down to a matter of focus. There are so many wonderful places to visit in this world. It's easy to get carried away and distracted when making your vacation plans. Having a bit of focus will bring clarity along with the perfect experiences for your family.

It may take some creative "backwards engineering" to make a dream come true. Say your dream is to take your family to Hawaii. You have one week to see as much as possible. Most people don't realize there are actually 137 Hawaiian Islands. Even if you were to focus on just the main tourist islands of Kauai, Oahu, Maui, Molokai, Lanai, and the big island of Hawaii, you would never hope to see everything in one short week. How do you prioritize? Often it requires aligning the answers of what type of vacation experience you want with your choice of destination to find the perfect match.

Say your family likes lots of action, big city excitement and nightlife, Honolulu on the island of Oahu has everything your family could ever want. If your family is looking for active adventures like hiking, quad bikes and zip lining, then Kauai may be the best fit. If your goal is for your kids to see a volcano up close, then the big island of Hawaii has it. If you simply want to kick back with your baby on a beautiful beach, Maui may be just right for you.

Your choice of destination may require additional focus in order to create a quality family vacation experience. With only one week of vacation, your family may not be able to see every country in Europe. Choosing one country or city would be a far more reasonable plan. If you are determined to see as much as possible, then perhaps a Mediterranean or river cruise might be a much better choice.

Similar experiences can be found in completely different destinations. Your six year old daughter may have a love affair with giraffes. Her dream is to interact with them in the wild.

Africa is a huge continent. If giraffes are your priority, start with a stay at the Giraffe Manor in Nairobi, Kenya. Here your daughter can interact and learn all there is to know about giraffes. Her new friends can even join her for breakfast every morning. With your priority as your starting point, it's easier to build your visit to South Africa from here.

Of course, you have to balance your choice of destination around your children's ages, travel styles, budget and abilities. A three hour flight to visit to the San Diego Zoo may be far more realistic when your giraffe-loving daughter is age two than having her endure a 22 hour flight. Save Africa as a destination until she is old enough to enjoy, appreciate and embrace everything it offers. It will make a much bigger impact on your child's life if you can also choose the right destination for the right age of your kids. It may also give you more time to save and budget accordingly.

Destination may not even be a high priority for your family. Perhaps you're traveling with your toddler for the first time. You may not be as particular about exactly where you want to spend your vacation. You simply want to find a fun spot that is less than a two hour nonstop plane ride from your home. It doesn't matter to you if you visit Walt Disney World or Disneyland. If you can survive the nonstop flight and your child gets to see Winnie the Pooh before turning three (when you'll have to pay to get into the park) then all is right with your world. This may be your family's first step to becoming true travelers.

There are also situations where your family's vacation destination has been predetermined. Perhaps the honor of your presence is expected at your sister's wedding and you need to find fun and engaging things for your kids to do during your stay in Jamaica.

5. HOW MUCH IS OUR VACATION BUDGET?

Ah money! The one thing most people prefer not to discuss and yet one of the most important factors when it comes to achieving their vacation dreams.

Ever notice, when lottery winners hit "the big one," one of the first things they tend to say is that they are going to "quit their job and travel the world." Most folks think they have to be a millionaire to take their family on a vacation. This simply isn't true.

If you wait until you think you can afford to travel, your dreams will simply remain on hold. Years from now you will look back and think "woulda, shoulda, coulda" instead of sharing stories of your amazing experiences. If you make travel a priority and set realistic goals, these dreams will come true.

Here is another shopping scenario that moms out there will certainly understand: you receive an invite to attend some fancy event. Perhaps it's a friend's wedding, company holiday party or charity event. You need to shop for that perfect "little black dress". Do you head to a fashion show in Milan, a designer boutique, Nordstrom or T.J.Maxx? Obviously the price points are all different but, bottom line, you'll still come home with that little black dress you crave and you will look amazing!

The same holds true for travel. Any destination or itinerary can be created using deluxe, moderate or value components. The bottom line is that your family gets to see the world while your kids experience amazing new adventures that will broaden their horizons.

The tricky bit is having a realistic idea of the cost involved. Use online travel websites to get some idea of airline tickets and hotel rooms as a reality check. Not a day goes by in our travel agency that we don't get a request from somebody wanting to take a last-minute family vacation with three teens to a luxury all-inclusive Caribbean resort for spring break week with a total travel budget of $1,000. Nope! Sorry, but that's simply unrealistic and is not going to happen. It might be possible to take a three night cruise to the Bahamas with that budget.

The biggest mistakes novice and DIY travelers make is not understanding how to do basic travel math!

In order to determine affordability and to figure out if you are getting the best value for your money, you have to compare every component of the trip. You must compare "apples to apples."

Travel agents can usually match or beat any advertised prices customers find on the Internet. This means customers get a low price and high quality customer care so it's the best of both worlds. To do a price match, travel agents always ask for a written price quote because 1) the trip must still be available for that price and 2) we need to compare "apples to apples"... are they the exact same flights? Same hotel room category? Does it include transportation? Your online "vacation deal" may be priced $100 cheaper than the price we gave you, but your "deal" does NOT include resort transportation, which will cost your family an additional $150 each way when you find yourself stranded at the airport. Now which deal is better? By comparing like with like and doing all the travel math it's soon obvious.

Here's another prime example: most folks would argue that renting a beach house for $2,500 per week for their family would be far cheaper compared to an exotic, Caribbean all-inclusive resort vacation. They would laugh and insist that their family could never afford that type of extravagance. The problem with this is that, again, it's not comparing like with like. They are simply comparing the cost of accommodation but forget all of the components in each itinerary.

So let's do the real travel math...

That "extravagant" Caribbean all-inclusive vacation costs $4,100 for their family of four. This price includes airport parking, airfare, round-trip transportation from the airport to your resort, all meals, snacks, room service, drinks (alcoholic and non-alcoholic), entertainment, non-motorized watersports, tips, taxes and even free child care.

To make a true and honest comparison to that beach house that you've been renting for $2,500 every summer, you would need to factor in the hard cost of $2,200 your family of four would ultimately be paying in addition to the house rent for gas, tolls, parking, beach permits, rides at the boardwalk, groceries, drinks, restaurants and tips. This would bring your total vacation cost for that "cheap" week at the beach to $4,700.

So let's review... $4,100 for a Caribbean all-inclusive resort where everything is done for you compared to the $4,700 cost of renting a beach house where you do all the work, driving and cleaning, as well as having to entertain the kids. Your family is still $600 ahead with that "extravagant," all-inclusive Caribbean vacation. Granted, if this is your family's first trip overseas, all four of you will need a passport which will cost approximately $100 each. Passports are good for the next 5-10 years depending on age. Even with the cost of passports figured in, you're still paying less for that "extravagant" Caribbean all-inclusive resort than that beach house rental down the shore.

Now which vacation do you think is truly better value?

Family vacations should be fun and relaxing for everyone. Fear and worry over finances is certainly NOT fun. If Dad goes ahead and books the perfect family vacation to Disney World that has a $4,000 price tag only to have Mom complain that they have saved only $2,000, there will certainly be friction. If they go ahead with their vacation but spend their time stressing about how they are going to pay the credit card bill, the trip won't be much fun for anyone. This is why there needs to be a frank and honest discussion about money in the early stages of planning a vacation.

In many cases, budgets can appear more manageable if you work backwards. Take a similar example: a $4,000 Disney vacation for two adults and two kids and let's see if we can avoid some arguments here...

Say the flights cost $350 per person and like most nonrefundable airfares, the airline tickets will need to be paid in full right up front. This means that $1,400 needs to be paid immediately to confirm their flights. Disney requires just a $200 deposit for their vacation packages that can include a stay at a Disney Resort, park admissions and even a meal plan. So this brings our immediate total amount due for the cost of the airline tickets and the Disney deposit to $1,600 (and Mom has enough in the bank by that date to cover this amount).

Disney needs to be totally paid 45 days prior to your arrival. If this family planned nine months in advance as suggested, this would allow six months to pay off their balance of $2,400 or $400 per month. This can be set up just like a store layaway program so that payments can be made in monthly installments.

So how can this family afford the monthly installment payments of $400? They still have $400 left in the bank to cover the first month's payment, which will give them a bit of a running start. If travel becomes a priority for your family, you'll be amazed at the many ways you'll find to fund your dreams. For example, recent statistics say that two-thirds of working Americans spend $37 a week buying lunch out and about $19 per week making coffee stops. If Mom and Dad agreed to simply brown bag it, that would instantly save $122 per week or $448 per month – more than enough to cover their Disney Vacation without any worry or credit card interest. It will actually create close to $300 in additional funds that they can use to splurge at Disney or save towards their next trip!

To determine a budget for your own family vacation dreams, the first step is to use the Internet to establish some realistic travel costs. Remember all the factors we've already discussed – start planning about nine months in advance and have the answers ready to your six guideline questions. Then go online to one of the large major travel websites and do a quick search to see how much the total cost of your vacation will be. This should take less than five minutes.

Often novice travelers suffer severe sticker shock when they see the cost of airline tickets, hotel rooms and cruise cabins. By putting together all these pieces of the travel puzzle, you should be able to come up with a realistic price tag for the vacation of your dreams. If you need to make your trip a bit more affordable, you will be able to easily see whether compromises can be easily made to obtain your goal. For example, maybe your destination will become more affordable if you stay fewer days or travel at a different time of year?

Next, find out the deposit amount due and when you will need to make the final payment. Every airline seat, hotel and vacation package has different rules and requirements. Often when you book travel online, you must pay for the entire trip in advance. At best, you will be required to pay a certain deposit amount with a final payment due X amount of days prior to your departure.

Travel agents offer different payment options so that you don't get caught paying credit card interest to the bank. They may also be able to suggest alternatives and compromises to help make your dreams attainable. Perhaps you have your heart set on vacationing at Atlantis resort in the Bahamas but the airfares and room rates are way over budget. A cruise to the Bahamas with a day excursion to Atlantis to swim with the dolphins and play at the water park may fit your budget perfectly with the bonus of including all of your meals.

Finally, look at your household budget. If you will have to finance your travel dreams, then first look for ways to save. This may mean cutting back on eating out, less spending on entertainment, selling unnecessary household "stuff" or even collecting loose change. If that still isn't enough, it may require a bit of overtime or a seasonal, part-time job to make it happen. Again, making a vacation a priority for your family will help set the right priorities and create a solid plan for reaching your dreams.

6. WHY TAKE THIS VACATION – WHY NOW?

Last, but probably most importantly, ask yourself honestly why are you taking this family vacation and why now? Finding your "why" will help you fine-tune all of your priorities and plans.

- Is your family celebrating an important milestone event – a landmark birthday, the end to chemo, grandparents' anniversary?

- Perhaps this vacation is a "babymoon" prior to welcoming a new member to the family?

- Is this the "last" family vacation together before your oldest heads off to college?

- Maybe your vacation is to honor, remember, or to fulfill the wish of a loved one?

- Grandma has been complaining that you're long overdue for a visit.

- You have practiced and trained to climb Mount Kilimanjaro? That is your mission and now is your time.

- Perhaps your family simply wants to embrace new adventures. The kids are old enough and you've all had a dream to learn how to scuba dive.

- Why do you want to visit Machu Picchu? Because it's there!

- Everyone just needs a week to chill on the beach!

There are a million correct answers to this question.

Your answer will help you in setting all of your travel priorities. If compromises need to be made, it will help you make the right choices.

For some novice travelers, your "why" may be to overcome your fear of travel. The thought of surviving a flight with a baby or toddler may seem inconceivable to many parents. The feeling of survival, achievement and accomplishment you feel as you deplane will make you feel invincible.

Often, not everyone in the family will have the same answers to the "why" question. It may take some creative diplomacy to get everyone on the same page.

A travel agent can often offer some creative problem solving and suggestions to vacation planning impasses. Recently I consulted with a couple who wanted a destination wedding in the Bahamas with family and friends. They were limited on travel dates due to their 19-year-old daughter's college exams and horrible flight schedules from Arizona. Instead of flying everyone to the Bahamas, we scheduled a cruise out of Fort Lauderdale. The bride and groom had their ceremony onboard the ship prior to sailing so that their daughter could attend. She then hopped a quick flight home to Arizona while the couple sailed off into the sunset with their guests.

Make sure the motives to your "why" are pure, honest and realistic. If your family or marriage has serious problems, an escape for a week in paradise is simply that, an escape. If your problems do not follow you there they will certainly be there to greet you the moment you get home. Vacations can certainly be fun, relaxing and inspiring, but they will not fix anything that is already broken.

Problems can also pop up as we share our "whys" with others. Tell a trusted friend that you plan to fly to Mexico with your baby and your "why" may quickly be turned into, "Why ever would you want to do that?" This response is usually followed by a barrage of negative remarks and negative comments that stomp on your dreams. This person may have never been to Mexico or even taken a vacation with their family, yet suddenly they become an expert. It's like sharing the happy news that you're pregnant and receiving a quick congratulations followed by incessant horror stories about labor.

Negative thoughts and pessimism surround us. Many times it comes from the people we love the most. It may be fear, guilt, brainwashing, inexperience, jealousy or a number of other factors behind their motives. Be alert to negative thinking and do not let it infect your fearless optimism. Whatever their reasons, do not let it affect your "why." Opening your heart to a world of possibilities will enlighten your mind and the minds of your kids. In the end, your vacation tales and adventures will often enlighten the minds of even the most negative naysayers.

With each year that passes, your family vacation "whys" may change, but your ultimate vacation "why" should be your children and turning them into better grown-ups someday. Opening your kids up to a world of possibilities will hopefully help them to remain more open, positive and fearless throughout their adult lives to come.

« Chapter Four »

TRAVEL AGENTS AS PARTNERS

Hopefully by now you appreciate why answering the six vacation guideline questions is so very important. You can see how the answer to each and every one these important questions impacts all of the others. These answers will give you guidelines, clarity and focus helping you to make the best decisions while making your vacation reservations.

Now what?

Even with your questions answered and razor-sharp focus, there are still an overwhelming amount of vacation choices available, especially if you turn your attention to vacation shopping online. Searching the millions of online choices and reading thousands of stranger reviews can quickly set you off on that endless hamster wheel journey to analysis paralysis.

Is this an efficient use of your time as a busy parent?

Even if you do find the perfect vacation of your dreams, there are often several different ways to purchase your trip. Would you save more money if you purchased your flights, hotels and transportation separately? Is it less expensive to purchase a complete vacation package? (Psst – the answer to this question may not be as obvious as you think).

Chances are you probably don't know what you think you know. For example, if you're taking a cruise, is it best to purchase your flights from the cruise line or should you book them separately? Do you know how to schedule your flights properly so as not to "miss the boat?" If you need to make a flight connection, how much time should you allow between flights at that particular airport?

Before you go and plunk down your credit card deposit, have you read all that tiny fine print in the terms and conditions of the travel contract you are about to enter? Better yet, do you fully understand how these rules may affect you and your family, as well as your finances?

Even if you do end up planning everything perfectly, what if something goes wrong? ...a flight connection is missed, a ship sails without you, your bags are lost, a storm threatens to ruin your trip, a volcano on the other side of the planet erupts – do you know how to adapt and handle these situations? Better yet, do you want to spend the time necessary to fix the situation?

Wouldn't you like to have somebody on your side watching out for you?

What if I were to tell you that you could have a trusted friend and ally on your team?

A professional advisor and trusted confidant, someone with firsthand travel knowledge with an expert eye for detail? Would you like to know someone who is at the ready to make your life and the lives of your family even easier? They would be armed with insider secrets and friends in important places. They would protect your family from harm and be ready to serve at your beck and call.

Believe it or not, this is not the description of your kid's favorite superhero... it's your travel agent.

Think of a travel agent as your personal tour guide through the vacation planning journey. A travel agent the experience, knowledge and expertise to customize and enhance your vacation experience while helping you avoid potential pitfalls, hassles and risks.

The sad fact is that most parents don't realize how much help, support and extra enjoyment a travel agent can add to your family's vacation. They don't understand how to work with a travel agent. They are convinced they can save themselves a ton of money if they do the work for themselves. People are often shocked when they realize how much additional value a travel agent can add to their enjoyment while saving hours of time and money from their bottom line.

Many parents fail to recognize how much their own time costs them. I've talked to many parents who will say, "I enjoy spending time searching for travel deals – it's like a hobby." Sure, but just how much is that time costing you and your family? Figure out how many hours of your time you're spending online looking for that vacation deal. On average, a simple family vacation takes a minimum of five hours of planning time. In my experience, I would say this time is mainly spent on transportation and lodging. Start coloring in the daily events, activities, dining, etc., and the clock keeps on ticking. Even at minimum wage, your time is worth a decent amount of money. Is it worth the frustration and confusion?

There is a very good chance that an experienced travel agent, one devoted to family travel, most likely would have an answer for you off the top of their head or in a matter of minutes. They "know" all this info or exactly where to find out because this is their profession. They practice their craft all day every day. All that time you spent searching online could have meant extra quality time spent with your children. Above all, the time we parents get to spend with our kids is priceless. So why waste it?

Hotels, cruise lines and tour companies factor the cost of travel agent commissions into the total price of their products. If you don't use the services of a travel agent, those extra profits are kept by the hotels, cruise lines and tour companies. You don't get any sort of refund for doing all the heavy lifting yourself. Why not take advantage and enjoy the services of a travel agent? You've already paid for it.

There are indeed those folks who really do take satisfaction in owning their travel planning. It's just like the folks who feel major satisfaction assembling their own IKEA furniture. It's that sense of pride, accomplishment and ownership. If you're this type of person, rest assured that you can still benefit greatly by collaborating with a travel agent. Your agent can review your plans to make sure they are both logistically and cost-effective. Agents can also contribute ideas, enhanced experiences and even local contacts that can help elevate your adventure to a whole different level of enjoyment. Having a professional travel agent watching over your shoulder means your family can anticipate a wonderful vacation with fearlessness and peace of mind.

Most travel agents will meet or even beat any advertised deals that you think you've found online. Travel agents also have rates and products available to them that are not found on any public online travel websites. They work with many different providers and can put together customized trips, again the kind that won't be found online. They know how to do travel math and can help you calculate all hard costs while comparing apples to apples. This ensures that you make the best and most informed decisions for your family. If they cannot meet your price, chances are what you have found is a scam or a situation that can potentially put your family at risk.

Some folks may still laugh and say, "Who needs a travel agent when I can book our trip myself online?" Those are the folks who have no idea of all the fun they're missing and the risks they are taking until it's often too late. Chances are these are the same folks who cut their own hair and then complain about bad hair days!

In today's busy world, parents need all the help and support they can possibly get. Hopefully something said here will help convince even those "type A" folks that a travel agent can be your best ally. If you still prefer to wear the cape and try to save the universe... may the force and availability be with you!

A travel agent works in a similar way to a real estate agent. If you were looking to buy a new home, you would present your wish list to your real estate agent. That agent would then present some homes for you to view, counsel you on your best options, assist you with all the financial paperwork, go over all the fine print to make sure you are making the best decision, help protect your interests with inspections and insurance, and hold your hand at every step of the process. At closing, the seller pays your real estate agent a commission.

The same scenario is pretty much true when it comes to vacation planning with a travel agent. Your travel agent will review the answers to your six questions: your family's unique needs and wish lists. In turn, they will present you with the best vacation options for your family. Hopefully your travel agent will have visited the destination and will have done personal inspections so that their advice comes from firsthand knowledge. Once you've decided on the perfect vacation plan, your agent will review all the fine print, go over payment plans, travel insurance and make sure your vacation investment is protected. Your agent will call on key contacts, help create the finer points of your daily itinerary, offer pre-departure tips, and hold your hand at every step of the way and answer any questions you may have. If you happen to encounter an unforeseen problem, you simply make one call to your travel agent who will get the situation sorted.

After you return home, your travel agent will be paid a sales commission from your hotel, cruise line or tour company. Notice that I did not include airline commission for travel agents. That is because airlines do not pay a sales commission to travel agents for airline tickets. The airlines stopped paying commissions years ago. This is why travel agencies that do still sell just simple plane tickets may charge a small service fee per ticket. They are charging for their time, overhead and their cost of doing business.

Whether you're working with a realtor or a travel agent, the value they bring is based on their expertise, their contacts and the time they are investing into your family's comfort and happiness. They act as your family's representative, ready to serve your best interests. Your agent is an ally to find the perfect house or vacation.

The part that most folks overlook is how important relationships are when it comes to traveling fearlessly. Agents base many of their recommendations on travel companies with longstanding reputations. Your agent knows that your family's safety and enjoyment demands traveling with reputable companies. This peace of mind may not come with the lowest price tag.

Making the right decisions from the start could save your bank account, not to mention hours of worry. Should something unforeseen happen, wouldn't it make you feel better knowing you have an expert on your side helping you make the right decisions and ready to champion your cause whenever necessary?

For example, a good real estate agent will have the inside scoop on some great deals that are simply not available to the general public. Your realtor might be friends with a contractor who is looking to quickly move a home they will be flipping over the next 30 days. Through this relationship, you may find and pay a deposit on the perfect house before it is ever seen in multiple listings. The real estate agent will help you negotiate and buy that house at a fair, comparable market value.

Good travel agents have the same sort of networks. Most will match any online sale prices (or explain any hidden risks). Most people don't realize that travel agents are often privy to sales, deals and special rates that are not listed on public travel websites. Their personal contacts can often get you perks that will enhance your stay, while saving you a great deal of time and aggravation. Some travel agents will watch your reservations and apply sale pricing even after you have made your initial deposits. This way you're guaranteed the best price even when you book far in advance.

Some travel agents may charge service fees. If you're not sure, just ask them. As mentioned previously, if they still sell plain old plane tickets, they may charge a small service fee for their time. Also, if you are asking a travel agent to plan a very detailed, complicated, customized itinerary or plan an event for a large group, they may ask for a service fee in advance. If so, be sure to get a signed agreement and know the terms of your relationship in advance.

Travel agents set these policies because their time is as valuable as yours. Let's face it, nobody wants to invest time working if they are not getting paid. Most agents will ultimately apply all or some of this service fee to your down payment or deposit when you confirm your reservations. Asking for a service fee up front is fair compensation for the time, knowledge and expertise they are investing on your behalf. To give you the best service, your travel agent may need to do professional research, invest significant time and may even need to pay the costs of overseas phone calls. Depending on the time difference, these contact calls may need to be made outside of normal business hours.

Now that you understand a bit more about the travel business and how to work with a travel agent, you'll see why families need a good agent on their side. It's different if you simply have to make travel arrangements for yourself. Traveling with children is a completely different story. When the safety and comfort of your most precious worldly possessions comes into play, it's an entirely different story.

If your boss tells you that your presence is required at a meeting in San Diego on a specific date, most of your six travel questions have already been answered for you. You need one airline seat to get you from your city to San Diego. Every hotel room in the world will accommodate one person. Even if it's not the best hotel in the world, you're only there for two nights so you can make the best of it. Unless your company has corporate travel contacts, these type of reservations are pretty straightforward.

The travel needs of any family are far more complicated simply because there are so many more needs and personalities involved. Let's use the same destination of San Diego as an example. First of all, if you're taking the kids along, you want the best hotel and the most value for your hard-earned dollars. Second, if it's for the whole week so you don't want to be stuck in some place less than adequate or you will never hear the end of it. How many hotels in San Diego will allow three kids ages 9, 13, and 15 to share the same room with their parents? You will also need to ask yourself questions like, "What will we be doing there every day? How will we all get around? Where are the best place to eat and will any accommodate my son's gluten free diet?"

Can you see how the travel needs change when it comes to family travel?

If you are a DIY travel planner going online to book your family's trip to San Diego, you may inadvertently see cheap airline tickets and book connecting flights without enough connection time in a very busy hub airport. Straight away this could cause a domino effect that could ruin your entire trip.

To maintain optimal profits, the airlines are consolidating many flights and routes. This means there are simply less flights available. This helps keep profits at a maximum level for the airlines, but if you miss your connection and need to rebook not just one, but five seats for your family, there's a good chance that you may have to wait a day or two days for enough seats to continue your journey.

Next, you may notice that there are few, if any, hotels available. You're not traveling at a peak holiday time and find this hard to believe. There may be plenty of hotel rooms, it may simply be that your family is the problem and it has to do with occupancy rules.

Every hotel maintains occupancy rules. These rules are based on local building codes, safety, liability and are in place to protect the comfort of all guests. For most hotels, occupancy rules will allow two adults and two children to share a room based on double adult occupancy. The defined age of a child may vary. For many hotels a child is considered to be under the age of 12. When the clock strikes midnight on your child's 12th birthday, they suddenly are charged adult hotel rates. In other cases, a particular hotel may define a child as someone under age 15 or even 18, it all depends. If most of the hotels in San Diego offer rooms based on two adults and two children under the age of 12, your family may not fit this definition on two counts. First of all you have three kids, not two and, secondly, two of those kids are over the age of 12. According to hotel rules, your family will be required to stay in two rooms. You will not all be allowed to share the same hotel room together.

But wait, there's more...

Remember that bit about "double adult occupancy?" This bit means the price of all hotels rooms is based on two adults sharing that room. If your two teens must stay in another room, this means they will be paying full adult rates. And that's not the worst of it... adjoining hotel rooms with a shared door are a request and never a guarantee. So not only will your family have to pay full rate for two hotel rooms, there is no guarantee that those rooms will be located anywhere near one another. Having your request honored is based on several factors, for example, whether the hotel offers adjoining rooms, availability at the time of check-in, and even whether or not the desk clerk is in a good mood.

A seasoned travel agent who is experienced with the special needs of families could immediately know how to solve many of these roadblocks. They would know to select nonstop flights or itineraries that offer longer connection times regardless of the cost. Preventing problems is cheaper than the time and money to correct travel mistakes.

In addition, that agent would be privy to hotel reservation systems that would allow them to find hotels offering guaranteed adjoining room categories. This means you would pay one price for two rooms that are absolutely connected. Another option may be apartment rentals that offer similar amenities at a comparable price with more space for a larger family. Once your basic travel arrangements are sorted, your agent can help find you the perfect restaurants and arrange for your daily activities and sightseeing. This will make your travels worry-free, organized and will save precious time standing around waiting to pay the price of admission to area attractions (which is usually higher when purchased separately).

Hopefully from these simple examples, it's clear how a travel agent can be a helpful ally when making vacation plans for your family. Just imagine if this was a complex itinerary or overseas tour. Time changes, language translation and cultural differences can all lead to potential problems. Having the help of an experienced travel agent can make all the difference.

Now that you appreciate the need for expert travel help, how do you go about finding the travel agent that is right for your family or particular journey? Going back to our earlier example, just like there are fabulous and really awful real estate agents, the same is true with travel agents.

Sadly, the only reward for some people is money. What they are looking for is a quick sale so that they can smile all the way to the bank. Travel companies are forever offering perks, freebies and incentives so that travel agents will sell their products over a competitor's. There are many times when parents will be "shopping around," and after a few minutes of discussion they share the recommendations they have received from other travel agents. This may not be the right fit for that family's particular needs but, knowing the current incentives offered by that property, it becomes immediately apparent why these other agents are eager to make this recommendation and sale. Selling this trip would benefit the travel agent instead of the family.

A good travel agent is more passionate about their client's needs than they are about making a sale. Travel is their business and any smart businessperson knows that, in order to be continuously profitable—now and in the future—it's all about investing in long-term relationships. If you over-deliver on making your clients happy they will not only return to you year after year, they will tell their family and their friends who in turn will do the very same. This is simply good business sense.

First things first: you want to find yourself not only a travel agent who has extensive travel experience but also one who specializes in the unique needs of parents traveling with kids of all ages. Family travel is a specialty and a separate niche market within the travel industry. If you were having a baby you would want to be treated by an obstetrician. You wouldn't get the special help you need by visiting a brain surgeon.

Next, ask if your travel agent has experience with or better yet, ask if they have visited your preferred destination, stayed in your selected resort, taken the same cruise, etc. I can't tell you how many times I've read reviews or seen photos of a particular vacation spot or hotel, only to visit it and find it's nothing like my expectation. Of course this can go either way; it can be far better than I anticipated or far worse. It might be a dream location for a particular type of family or a nightmare for others. But, obviously, firsthand experience is vital to making the right travel plans. You do want to make sure your personal travel agent has the right kind of experience that will best suit the needs of your family.

Not every travel agent, even those who specialize in family travel, can see and do everything. Just when we agents know every single minute detail about a particular destination or vacation, it changes. New rules, upgrades and experiences happen all the time in the travel biz. Of course travel agents want to build long-term relationships with their families. Still, what is most important is ensuring that our families get the latest information and the very best service possible. This is why, in our agency, we work as a team. Each of our agents specializes in different areas of family vacations – Disney, Caribbean, Europe, Hawaii cruises, etc. If one of our clients is better served by another of our members for a particular vacation, we refer them to that expert.

Hopefully your agent really listened to you, spent some time and truly understands your family's vacation wishes. When presented with your agent's itinerary choices, do not just accept them at face value. Ask your agent why they chose a specific ship or resort. What were the reasons behind their selections? Hopefully all of their decisions will address your family's specific needs and wishes as outlined by your six questions. This is a good way to judge whether they have your best interests at heart.

The best way to build an alliance is through trust. The long list of rules, regulations, updates, laws, scams, foreign regulations and more could fill volumes of books. The reality is that most people don't care about all of these issues. Most parents simply want the most vacation fun for the lowest price. As mentioned earlier in our discussions about budgets, people are often reluctant to talk freely about money.

Please treat your travel agent as your partner – not your adversary. It's all about mutual respect, collaboration and team work. That's how long-standing relationships happen.

Don't think you're being "slick" when it comes to shopping online for vacations. Every travel agent expects that clients have done online vacation shopping. Keep honest lines of communication open and let your travel agent know about your findings. Honesty is in YOUR best interest. If you happen to find a lower price than the one for the trip your agent is recommending, you both can discuss the differences openly. Your price may be offered by a company that your travel agent knows is on the brink of bankruptcy. This knowledge could potentially save you a world of hurt.

Your travel agent is human. They do not own a crystal ball. With millions of flights, hotels, local sales and social media promotions, occasionally parents will find a cheaper price themselves online. Normally your agent can book your trip for you at the lower price or explain why you may be taking a risk booking at this low rate. You get the best price, their extra service, their contacts, their expertise and they still get paid for the time they have invested on your behalf. Open communication is a win-win for everybody.

Sure, you may be able to book the same hotel yourself and save a few pennies. You may not realize that the "deal" you found will require you to spend several hours of your precious vacation as the victim of a high-pressure timeshare sales presentation. Maybe the cheaper price you've found doesn't include features like airport transportation or insurance, which will leave you more out of pocket in the long run.

Here's another potential pothole that your travel agent can help you avoid when it comes to hotel reservations. Hotel rooms can be bought in many different ways. A guest can go online and book their own hotel room online, they can call the hotel for reservations, or they can work with a travel agent. In most cases, travel agents will work with a wholesale travel company. These are companies that obtain contracts from airlines, car rental companies and hotels to create vacation packages.

Good and fair business practices would dictate that hotels offer the same price for their rooms regardless of how that reservation was made. Of course different channels of distribution have different costs of doing business. Ultimately the goal of every hotelier is to put the most "bums into beds" at the highest possible profits. "Bums" is certainly not meant to be a derogatory term here. It is an informal industry term derived from Europe to describe one's backside. Here in the states, we'd say "butts into beds." Bottom line (pun intended), meaning to fill hotel rooms and make the most profits possible.

Selling rooms directly to the customer is the quickest way for a hotel to reap the most profit. Many hotels will offer their cheapest prices directly via their own reservation systems or websites. Of course, consumers are enticed by the lower prices and will book directly.

Travel agents know this can lead to serious problems. That is why most travel agents will book with a large wholesaler. These companies book millions of dollars of travel every year. They are big players. Without their worldwide distribution systems, many hotels would be stranded with lots of empty rooms. It may cost a little bit more for hoteliers to work with wholesalers, but it is worth it in the long run.

Many unsuspecting travelers are not aware of some of the business practices hoteliers use to increase their profit margins. Most hotel chains have a sophisticated algorithm in place to predict their yields or ultimate profits. In simple terms, they play the Vegas odds. Hoteliers, especially those located in high demand tourist spots, will purposely oversell. They will take more reservations than they have space. The idea here is that on any given night, a certain number of travelers will cancel for one reason or another. Just like Vegas, there are no sure winners when you play the odds.

Folks are often surprised when they show up at a hotel after a long journey only to find there is a problem with their reservation. When a hotel is overbooked, they will "walk" customers to another local hotel. This hotel may or may not be convenient or meet your family's needs. So, when a hotel is overbooked and the decision needs to be made to "walk" guests, who do you think will be the first guests chosen and sent packing? It's the guests who have paid the lowest rates to stay at that hotel. Usually these are the people who booked direct or bid a low rate at an online auction.

Travel agents know all about these tactics, and that is why they normally will chose to work with a wholesale company which carries a lot of industry clout. Hoteliers normally will not walk wholesaler clients for fear of ruining a very lucrative distribution channel. That is why paying a few pennies more at the start and making your reservations through the right channels is a much better investment when it comes to your family's comfort and peace of mind.

In another scenario, let's say your family arrives at a perfectly wonderful resort that just so happens to be host to a wild bunch of foreign conventioneers. The hotel managers, security and local authorities are doing everything possible to keep the peace but it is simply not a good environment for young children. If you've booked directly with that resort, do you think the hotel wants to lose your revenue by moving you to a competitor's hotel down the road? No matter how angry you are and how much you threaten the desk clerk, they have your money and you are a captive audience. If your agent booked you through a wholesale tour company, local representatives from that tour company would help to move you to a much more appropriate environment for your kids so that you could all enjoy the rest of your vacation.

Once again, your travel agent is there as your representative and advisor. They can help ensure that you not only get the best price and the best value when making your family's vacation reservations, they want to ensure that you are treated fairly. By making the best decisions from the start, you can avoid costly and unnerving problems during your trip.

« Chapter Five »

SIX STAGES OF FAMILY VACATIONS THROUGH THE AGES

Your family's travel and vacation needs evolve every few years. This means your vacation planning needs to change and adapt to the needs of your family as it grows.

There are some families that will take "traditional" vacations to the exact same spot year after year. Maybe they own a vacation home or rent a place the second week of July every year. Whether they travel with a baby or college kids, this family "adapts" their lifestyle to fit their vacation environment. Everyone knows exactly what to expect and there is no risk. Chances are the people who are content with this type of vacation scenario are not reading this book.

Family vacations should inspire and enlighten everyone in the family regardless of age or life stage. Previous chapters of this book discussed the Six Important Questions we need to ask ourselves every year when we start to do travel planning for a family vacation – who, what, where, when, why and how much.

In keeping in theme with the number six, there are also six life stages that most parents will "grow" through with their children:

1. Pregnancy

2. Baby

3. Toddlers

4. School-age kids

5. Tweens

6. Teens

Each of the six family life stages has particular travel issues and priorities that need to be recognized and addressed. Understanding the travel needs for families during each of these different life stages allows travel agents to customize a vacation that is the perfect fit for your family – instead of making your family fit a typical vacation.

Of course there is life after kids as parents become a couple of empty nesters and eventually grandparents. Your family is also part of an extended family. Also other life events like death and divorce influence vacation planning. We will touch on these topics in later chapters but, for now, understanding these six stages of family life will help us to really customize new vacation experiences.

The needs of a pregnant mom will obviously be very different than when she takes her little bundle of joy on that first airplane ride. A flight will be different for a first-time parent compared with the parents with older children who have more parenting experience.

This part of the book will focus on some unique travel situations that every family will face over time. By taking these life stage factors into consideration right in the early planning stages, a fun and memorable time will be had by everyone. It's all about finding the right vacation fit at the right time in your life. It's like finding the right pair of shoes... if you don't have the right fit there will be blisters, and nobody likes blisters!

Fearless Family Vacations

A great family vacation is balanced, fun and fair for everyone. Chances are most families will travel with members at a variety of different life stages. For example, a young couple with a new infant may be vacationing along with grandparents and a teen "uncle." By understanding the unique travel needs of everyone in the family, itineraries can be customized and geared for all ages.

If you are the parents of, for example, an eight- and a six-year-old, you will probably be tempted to page ahead to read about what affects your family at this stage and time in your lives, as well as what lies ahead. That is completely understandable, of course. That said, learning how to travel is a bit like using building blocks. Tips and ideas from earlier chapters will certainly be helpful and perhaps spark ideas; so do make some time to read all of this info when can. Chances are it will also be good advice that you can pass along to other parents in need of a vacation. (Better yet – share a copy of the book with them. Thank you for allowing me this shameless plug!)

PREGNANT MOMS

Pregnancy is certainly a very exciting time for any family. Obviously the health and safety of both mom and baby are paramount. There can also be a bit of fear and anxiety, especially for brand new parents.

Years ago women used to stay close to home during the "confinement" of pregnancy. Thankfully times have changed dramatically. One of the most popular trends in family travel is the babymoon. This is when pregnant moms or couples plan a vacation prior to the birth of their new child. It's considered to be a "last hurrah" before 2 a.m. feedings and diapers. A massage at the spa or breakfast in bed is a nice splurge considering the road ahead.

Travel during pregnancy is all about timing!

Of course it's been mentioned here that parents should start making their family vacation plans nine months in advance. Even the best made plans can be interrupted by a surprise visit from the stork! This is why travel protection insurance is so very important. It protects both your health, as well as your vacation investment. This way, if the stork does pay your family a surprise visit, you'll be able to cancel or postpone your vacation. Without proper travel protection coverage, you could be potentially be risking the entire cost of your trip. Typical travel insurance coverage costs approximately 8 to 10% of the total cost of your vacation.

"Cancel for Any Reason" often works best for family vacations. This type of coverage does tend to cost a few pennies more but it certainly is something to consider as a protection should the stork pay your family a surprise visit.

With typical travel insurances, cancellations are only allowed if you meet certain criteria governed by the rules of the policy. For example, if you say you are ill, your doctor must collaborate with a written letter of documentation. If you have "Cancel for Any Reason" coverage there are no questions asked. The decision to cancel your trip is entirely up to you with no questions asked.

The reason why this is so very important when it comes to pregnancy is because most travel insurance coverages will list pregnancy as a "pre-existing condition" in their policy fine print. This means that pregnant moms may not be covered for cancellation. Read all fine print, ask plenty of questions and make informed decisions to avoid any surprises.

Checkup – Your first bit of travel planning should be a prenatal visit to your obstetrician. Get the green light from your doctor before you go anywhere. Your doctor knows you, your baby and your health best, so be sure to include your doctor in your decision-making process. Inform your doctor of precisely where you'll be traveling, especially if you're planning to travel outside of the US. Some foreign countries may require special vaccinations that may or may not be safe during pregnancy.

In addition, your doctor and medical staff can also offer advice and health support that will make you far more comfortable while on the road. Be sure to get any extra prescriptions you may need or suggestions regarding over-the-counter medications you may need.

It's also a good idea to create a medical file that you can take with you. Ask your obstetrician for a copy of your prenatal history. Create a worksheet that includes copies of your hospital and travel insurance policies. Make a contact list of names, phone numbers and email addresses of people you'd like contacted in case you need any emergency medical care or go into early labor. Include a copy of your birth plan and the direct dial phone number of your obstetrician. If you're traveling overseas, be sure you know the number of the local hospital, US Embassy and how to telephone home from either a landline or your cell phone in case of emergency.

Smart Scheduling – If you can plan your pregnancy and your travels, do try to plan your trip for your second trimester of pregnancy, from about 13 weeks to 24 weeks pregnancy. This is the time you're likely to be feeling your best. During the first trimester, morning sickness can cause problems which can be compounded by traveling. During the last trimester, size can cause general discomfort, back pain and foot swelling not to mention complications like high blood pressure and premature labor.

Airlines do have restrictions regarding pregnant mothers. Obviously there is a risk to mother and child if labor happens at 30,000 feet. The airlines are simply not equipped to handle this type of situation so they try to avoid the possibility. If a flight would need to be rerouted due to a potential delivery this also affects the lives and schedules of fellow passengers.

Most airlines do not allow pregnant first-time moms who are more than 36 weeks pregnant onboard their aircraft (32 weeks for moms of multiples). In addition, most airlines will require a letter from your obstetrician signed within 48 hours prior to your flight giving you medical permission to fly. Without a permission letter, they have the right to "deny boarding." Travel insurance will also not cover you in a situation where you don't follow the rules. You would lose the cost of your ticket. Of course, every airline has different rules and procedures that can be updated or changed. Be aware of these regulations. Do your homework online, ask your travel agent, question the airline and be an informed passenger.

These rules can create awkward situations at check-in. Some moms may look very pregnant early in their pregnancy while others may have an easy-to-camouflage, little baby bump right up until delivery. It's the job of every airline or cruise ship employee to enforce the rules and protect the health and safety of all passengers. Some check-in staff may approach the question of "exactly how pregnant you are" more delicately than others. Being an informed passenger who knows the rules and is prepared with your doctor's permission letter can help to avoid embarrassment for all.

Flying When Pregnant

When it comes to flying while pregnant, size matters in another way too. Most large, commercial aircraft are completely pressurized. Altitude will not have any effect on your or your baby. Smaller aircraft, especially those that fly at lower altitudes used for island-hopping or connecting outlying airports may not be fully pressurized. Under normal circumstances a short flight in these conditions is fine. With a pregnant mom, it could mean less oxygen getting to your little one.

Many airlines will allow you to reserve your airline seat ahead of time. Many pregnant moms prefer aisle seats close to a bathroom. Others prefer bulkhead seats that offer a bit more legroom. Pregnant moms are not allowed to sit in wider exit rows. While flying, it's best to stay seated with your seat belt fastened low across your hips and below your bump. If you do get up to use the toilet, be sure to hold on. Remember your center of gravity is not really centered and a little bit of turbulence can really send you flying and not in a good way!

Pregnant women are considered at high risk for DVT. Deep vein thrombosis (DVT) is a fancy name for blood clots, especially in the legs. DVT can be caused by long periods of inactivity, which causes a slowing of circulation that in turn leads to blood clots. Clots in the legs can cause pain and inflammation. The real risk is that one of these clots could break off, travel to the heart, lungs or brain causing life threatening situations, namely heart attacks and strokes. The risk for DVT increases if you are seated in a tight airline seat for a long flight, or even a long car ride. Exercise frequently throughout your flight and you feel better. Exercises also help avoid swelling ankles, slowing circulation and DVT. Simple stretches, frequent changes of position and even the tightening and relaxation of different muscles will help. You may want to ask your doctor about the use of special hosiery that can help circulation while easing the risk of DVT.

Cruising While Pregnant

Cruise ships also have rules in place for pregnant moms. Generally, pregnant mothers are not allowed to sail past 24 weeks of pregnancy. In addition, a letter of permission from your doctor may also be required. Cruise lines have these rules in place to ensure your safety and the convenience of all passengers. Even though cruise ships have doctors and medical staff onboard, again it's a matter of having proper medical attention for both mom and baby when you are far from land hospitals.

There are a few other issues pregnant moms need to consider when cruising. The motion of the ocean can aggravate symptoms of morning sickness. As mentioned earlier, timing matters so you may want to avoid sailing in your first trimester when morning sickness is usually at its worst. As your baby bump gets bigger it affects your balance and stability. Add the motion of the ocean to this situation and the risk of falls and injury can increase. Always hold onto railings and wear non-slip, stable shoes to avoid injury to you and your little one.

Hotels for Pregnant Moms

Hotel stays for pregnant moms should be all about comfort and convenience. Get the best location and the greatest luxury you can afford. Pregnancy is most certainly the right vacation life stage to splurge on hotel upgrades. If you hate parting with hard-earned dollars, think of it this way – you're traveling for two. Spending a bit more on upgraded features is like getting a "buy on/get one" deal for you and the baby.

Instead of opting for the basics of stairs and a lumpy bed at Motel 6, spend the money to stay at a real hotel with elevators a bellboy. Tipping him to carry your luggage will be money well spent after a tiring day of travel. Your cankles will thank you for it! Many upscale hotels have pillow menus and even spa services specially designed for pregnant moms.

Choosing a hotel in a convenient location can mean less stress and aggravation. It is extremely important for both your health and the baby to maintain proper nutrition while away from home. Be sure to select a hotel that offers good restaurant choices or is located near healthy restaurants that either deliver or are located nearby. Many hotels will offer refrigerators either upon request or for a small fee. This may also be a great option for keeping healthy snacks or to store water, juices and milk to help prevent dehydration.

Travel Tips for Pregnant Moms

Be Travel Wise – Do your best to travel light in order to avoid having to carry heavy bags. If not, it's better to tip a porter while navigating the airport. Ask for help when lifting bags. This is not the time to play superwoman! Play the pregnant card if you have to and ask for a seat on the bus if you must. It's best to save your strength and protect yourself from injury and harm than to suffer the consequences of being stubborn later on.

A couple of inflatable pillows may come in handy to help you stay comfortable during long seated periods. A tiny bottle of hand sanitizer can go a long way to keep you and your baby healthy while traveling. Remember to use it often. Keep your vitamins and any medications that you may need into your carry-on bag along with plenty of water to remain hydrated. When flying, you will need to purchase water after passing through airport security in order to comply with the 3-1-1 rule of three ounces or less in a one quart Ziploc bag. Do not assume that the airline staff will be serving drinks onboard and make sure you have enough water with you for your flight. Make healthy drink choices like fruit juices when offered and avoid caffeine when possible, but especially soda, which can lead to stomach discomfort.

The same is true with eating. Check in advance to see if your airline will be offering meal service on for your flight. Many airlines no longer serve meals, even on long flights. They will offer expensive snack boxes with less than healthy choices. Take along pre-packaged meals and extra snacks to nibble in case of any flight delays. Small frequent snacks instead of a heavy meal prior to your flight may help to alleviate bloating. Eating a high-fiber diet may also help prevent constipation, especially if you're taking prenatal vitamins with iron.

Fashion Statements – First and foremost, be comfortable while traveling! Wear relaxed, comfortable clothing and slip-on shoes. Remember you will need to remove your shoes at airport security so easy slip-on shoes with good support are best, especially if you can't see your feet any longer! Choose socks that will either support circulation or, at the very least, not restrict it should your ankles start to swell. If you're traveling to a tropical destination, wear cotton clothing and underwear. Don't sit in wet bathing suits as pregnant moms are more prone to yeast infections.

Common Sense – Use your head when it comes to your adventures and activities during your babymoon. Let's face it, bungee jumping or parasailing may not be your best vacation choices while pregnant. Be sun smart and play it safe. If you're active and healthy you certainly don't need to be a wallflower, but swimming with sharks may not be your best choice when you're traveling for two. Do try to maintain your usual exercise program and good eating habits to stay healthy. Be sure to include lots of downtime for rest and relaxation. This is certainly the best time for you to pamper yourself.

Good Nutrition – Healthy eating while away from home is also paramount. Again, select a hotel that offers restaurant, food and beverage services or one that is located conveniently near healthy restaurant and market choices. Remember to increase your fluid intake, especially with long flights or if traveling to hot, tropical climates.

Just because you are pregnant, that doesn't mean you have to stay locked away at home. However, you will need to time your travel appropriately and you will need to pace yourself to prevent exhaustion. Opt for a relaxing beach vacation, a visit to the spa, or the kind of trip where you are waited on like a queen. Do not cram your itinerary with back-to-back sightseeing. Allow yourself time to put your feet up and rest. Unless you are really accustomed to daily, vigorous exercises, save extreme sports for another trip. With a new baby on the way, you are embarking on the adventure of a lifetime. Use this trip to celebrate this wonderful new experience.

VACATIONS WITH BABY

For many new or first time parents, a nearby outing, or even a trip to the mall requires the logistics of planning a large scale military maneuver. The thought of taking a vacation with a new baby may sound completely overwhelming. It's okay! If you can make it to the mall and back with everything your little one needs, then you have all the skills necessary to take a vacation with your baby. No doubt, you probably need a vacation by now anyway.

The next argument that usually arises is that new parents don't want to feel like "those people" in public. You know, "those people" with the screaming child, disrupting everyone in the restaurant, while folks point, stare and criticize their parenting skills. Again, the good news is that—if you choose the right destination and surroundings for your vacation—no doubt you'll be surrounded with plenty of other parents who will understand, sympathize and be supportive of your plight as new parents.

Many new parents will say they will "wait until their baby gets older and more manageable before they plan a family vacation" but fail to realize how mobile babies can truly be. With each stage of their child's life, these procrastinating parents find a multitude of reasons to sit tight for years of staycations instead of embracing all the benefits travel offers their family.

Generally, all of the negativity that comes from traveling with a baby usually stems from fear of the unknown. Often, parents simply lack answers to their "how to" questions. Knowledge is power which, in turn, will build confidence. Once parents realize that planning a vacation with baby can easily be done, it opens up a world of possibilities for them.

Becoming new parents, albeit joyful, is accompanied by many new emotions. Exhaustion, a sense of separation from their "old" life and lack of freedom are emotions that can all add to the stress new parents experience. Taking a break from all of your worries, even a short break, will certainly help to recharge your batteries. It will help you take on your new roles as parents with new vitality and conviction.

Travel can be a wonderfully stimulating adventure for your baby too. It will help build your bond together with new experiences and memories. It will help your children become more flexible and adaptable as they grow. Travel is a life skill and it is never too early to learn.

Fearless parents who travel and vacation with their babies find that each trip gets easier and more fun. Procrastinating parents and their offspring never learn proper travel skills and etiquette. Travel to them means a world of worry instead of a world of wonderful possibilities.

Getting Started

Obviously health, safety and comfort become paramount when it comes to traveling with a baby. Who better to offer instruction and advice on keeping your baby safe and healthy while traveling than your baby's doctor? Your pediatrician knows your child's specific health history and can offer advice on how to keep baby healthy while traveling.

Even healthy infants do not yet have a fully mature immune system because they haven't received their full course of immunizations. It's true that antibodies from mom can help babies that are breastfed. Still, travel to certain destinations can put babies at considerable risk when it comes to communicable diseases. In some cases, your doctor may advise against traveling to certain destinations until your child is a bit older. Obviously, it is best to have this information before making any vacation plans as it will certainly save you time, money and aggravation.

Call or speak to your pediatrician before you begin planning your trip or confirm any vacation plans with your travel agent. This is even more important if your child has any health issues or complicated health history. This way you will avoid any last-minute disappointments or hassles.

Schedule a "travel" appointment with your pediatrician at least four to six weeks prior to your departure. Depending upon your specific itinerary and destination, travel immunizations may be required and can take several weeks to take effect. There may be certain diseases like yellow fever, measles, and meningococcal meningitis that may be a threat to infants. Small infants may be at risk because they are too young to be immunized.

Besides giving you the green light, your pediatrician or their nursing staff will be able to offer you specific travel advice. They can address concerns about topics like jetlag, sleeping or feeding schedules, motion sickness or any other specific health issues that may affect your family while you're traveling with your baby.

Perhaps "Murphy's Law" should be a motto for parenthood. It states, "Whatever can go wrong, will go wrong and at the worst possible time." One shouldn't be pessimistic but, as a parent, it's better to prepare for the worst possible scenario. If you are prepared, you will find yourself pleasantly surprised whenever things go smoothly and according to plan. For this reason parents should go to their doctor's visit prepared with a list of travel questions. They should make a list of all the possible health issues that could affect their little one during their trip. Ask the doctor for a list of recommended dosages for over-the-counter medications that may be needed during the trip... medications for jetlag, fever, bug bites, sun protection/burn, or tummy troubles, for example. Chances are, if you are prepared with the proper products and knowledge, you won't need them. Having this knowledge in hand could help you avoid an emergency room visit, let alone frustration while you're on the road.

It's also a good idea to keep a written copy of your pediatrician's direct dial phone number with you. Many 800 phone numbers will not work from certain countries or calling areas. If you're traveling to a foreign country, learn how to call back to the United States just in case you need to contact your pediatrician for an emergency. Your doctor may be able to suggest a pediatrician or preferred hospital at your destination. This way, in case any emergencies arise, you will have confidence about where to go for care. If your child is on prescription medications, you may want to get a copy of that prescription to keep with you while you travel. This way if something should spill or get broken, you can get it refilled locally.

Besides medical care, ask your pediatrician about any feeding advice for your baby while traveling. Breastfeeding while on a family vacation with your baby can be much easier than formula feeding. Maternity leave is one of the rare times in life that many moms are able to take extended time off from work. It's an excellent opportunity to take a vacation. Lactating moms have a portable solution to give their child all the nutritional requirements nature intended while providing a constant and familiar source of comfort. Even so, there are a few considerations you may want to take into account before leaving home. If you a heading to a warm or tropical destination, you may want to ask your pediatrician about offering extra fluids to your child to avoid dehydration.

If you are only breastfeeding your child, then you have no worries about sterilizing bottles or the availability of clean water. If you are supplementing with formula then this is a great time to splurge on ready-to-feed bottles or prepared canned formula. Be warned that changes in water used to mix formula may upset your baby, not to mention tap water in some travel destinations may not be fit to drink. Remember, babies have strong swallowing reflexes so be extra careful when bathing or swimming with your child in areas where the water may be in question. Generally breastfed babies have a lower incidence of getting traveler's diarrhea.

Traveling breastfeeding moms need to be mindful of their eating, sleeping and stress patterns as this could affect their breast milk production. This is a time to ask and accept help. Make life as easy as possible for yourself and avoid stress whenever possible.

If you and your child will be flying, you may want to consider using a baby sling. Baby slings offer a handsfree way to carry baby through the airport and while providing nursing privacy.

Infants have immature Eustachian tubes in their ears, which are very sensitive to air pressure changes. Swallowing can help balance the pressure in your child's inner ears so allow your child to nurse during takeoffs and landings. Security X-ray screenings have no effect on lactation, breastfeeding or breast milk. Breast milk does not need to be declared at customs. If you plan to carry expressed breast milk onboard, it's prudent to check with the latest airport security rules. Rules regarding the transport of liquids onboard aircraft are subject to change and should be checked prior to travel. Breast pumps are considered to be personal items and are subject to the same carry-on rules as other carry-on bags. Just be sure to check with your airline regarding size and weight restrictions to avoid additional baggage fees.

As far as accommodation is concerned, you may want to consider having access to a kitchen, or at least a refrigerator. This will certainly make life a bit easier if you plan to express or store your breast milk. Refrigerated milk can be frozen, but once frozen milk has been fully thawed, it cannot be re-frozen and it must be used within one hour. Expressed milk should be kept cool and stored in clean, tightly sealed containers. Use containers with tight seals that can be properly cleaned with hot, soapy water. If you are unsure of the water safety in your destination, sterilize containers with boiled water Many breastfeeding moms can easily pump manually and may find this more convenient while traveling. Others prefer electric pumps. If you need nursing support or equipment rentals while traveling, try contacting an international board-certified lactation consultant or the La Leche League.

As a traveling mom, please bear in mind that opinions on breastfeeding vary greatly. Some people consider it natural and totally acceptable while some places have laws forbidding it. Many developing countries associate breastfeeding with a lower economic status and less educated class of people. In some cultures, it is considered socially acceptable to admire and even interact with a nursing child. Airports can be interesting social bubbles because here you'll find a cross section of so many different cultures. Be respectful, learn, share experiences and try not to react to negative responses. When in doubt, it's usually best to be as conservative as possible. Do your best to find a private area to breastfeed your baby. Try to be as prepared as possible with clothing and covers for modesty. To enjoy cross-cultural experiences is often the reason we leave home in the first place, seeking adventure... and let's face it, parenthood is one of the greatest adventures of our lives. As travelers, and especially as parents, we are ambassadors, and we should strive to set a positive example through understanding and tolerance.

Most importantly, be confident. Perhaps the idea of a family vacation with your baby is REALLY enticing, but you're still fearful of how it will all work out. Try taking some baby steps!

Instead of planning some big weeklong adventure far from home, plan a short break or weekend getaway. Limit your travel time to either a one-hour flight or two-hour car trip, and stay one or two nights away from home. Visit family and friends or travel with family and friends if you really need moral support. Often, parents are pleasantly surprised at how flexible their babies are while traveling. Parents are often pleased to recognize how reality is far more fun than their fearful imaginations.

Once you've experienced a successful weekend away from home, you'll appreciate that a longer, well-deserved vacation is totally possible.

Flying with Your Baby

Can babies fly for free? The short answer is... yes. "TECHNICALLY" babies and toddlers under the age of 24 months can fly for "free." Airlines and travel agents use the industry word "LAPCHILD" to describe a baby or toddler flying seated in their parent's lap. Everyone likes the idea of a "free ride" but there are some VERY important points parents need to consider when deciding whether or not to buy an airline seat for their baby. Parents need to be informed so that they can make the best decisions regarding their child's safety, as well as their finances.

The Federal Aviation Administration (FAA) sets the standards for airline safety in the United States. The FAA does recommend that all children fly seated in an approved child safety seat, BUT... it does not MANDATE the use of child safety seats for babies on airplanes. The word "mandate" is an important one here. Because the FAA does not mandate the use of a safety seat, airlines WILL allow children UNDER the age of two to fly "FREE" seated in the lap of an adult.

We use the word "free" here in quotes because technically, a seat for a lapchild is never 100% free. Most airlines charge a small fee, usually 10% the cost of an adult ticket. And Uncle Sam never gives you a free ride when it comes to paying taxes. Nevertheless, the airfare for a lapchild under the age of two is significantly less than other passengers.

The airlines, the FAA, the National Highway Traffic Safety Administration (NHTSA) and concerned parents have been debating this issue for years. The NHTSA also comes into the discussion because they are the governing body responsible for rating and maintaining a list of approved, crash-tested car seats. The FAA and the airlines argue that airline travel is statistically far safer than driving a car. The fear is that requiring parents to buy an additional airline ticket for their baby may be cost-prohibitive for many families. This would in turn force more families putting more children at risk in auto accidents.

As a travel industry professional, I am often asked my opinion on the matter. As mentioned earlier in this book, most airlines cut sales commissions to travel agents back in the 90's. Whether you buy an airline ticket for your baby or not has no economic effect on most travel agent professionals.

Therefore, speaking as a travel agent, it doesn't really matter to me whether you buy an extra plane ticket or not. The point to be made here is that no travel agent is going to receive any huge economic gain by suggesting that you buy an airline seat for your baby.

Speaking as the mother of three kids and a former pediatric nurse, I wholeheartedly believe that **ALL** babies and children should be seated in an airline-approved car-safety seat, buckled into their very own airline seat. I have personally been onboard a plane that experienced turbulence at 30,000 feet. Although this is a very rare occurrence, it did result in numerous injuries to fellow passengers. Luckily I always keep my seat belt fastened in flight, but several passengers had to be taken off the aircraft on stretchers when we finally landed.

Turbulence can happen and often does without any warning. It can catch you off guard. It is my humble opinion that the most loving parent in the world cannot hold and protect their child seated in their lap against the g-forces of a jet flying over 500 mph that suddenly hits turbulence.

Once again, speaking as a mom, I too have had many challenges balancing our family's checkbook so I do understand both sides of this story. To help parents make an informed decision about whether or not to purchase an airline seat for their baby, let's consider the pros, cons and compromises...

PROS...

Fly Right – The FAA publishes an article and brochure for parents outlining child safety on airplanes. A simple Google search will help you find it online. Parents will find full details and I would urge you to heed their advice. Be sure your child's car seat is one that is approved for airline travel. Check to make sure this detail is printed somewhere on your child's car seat. Double-check that your child is the appropriate size for the seat you plan to use and be familiar with the instructions and operation of your child safety seat. If you have any remaining questions, reach out to your car seat manufacturer for product information and installation instructions. Securing and operating a child's safety seat is the responsibility of parents, not the flight crew.

Discounts – Many airlines do offer discounts for children so be sure to ask when making your reservations. Generally discounts offered are around 75% of the adult fare, but every bit counts. Keep in mind many big online travel websites may not offer child discounts via their public online reservation systems. This is another situation when using the services of a travel agent can help .

Airline Seating – Be aware that airline regulations require that child safety seats be placed in window seats in a non-exit row.

CONS....

Is Free REALLY Free? – Each and every airline has its own specific rules when it comes to lapchildren and how they need to be documented. Often there is a service or ticketing fee, which can average 10% of the adult airfare. Foreign airport taxes and fees may also need to be paid for "free" lapchildren. Be sure to ask, especially if you book your own airfare online. Many large online travel websites do not calculate these extra charges, and parents find themselves unpleasantly surprised at the airport check-in desk. Also, for foreign flights, remember ALL children, even those flying free as a lapchild, will always still need a passport. Don't forget to factor the cost of obtaining a new passport for your child into your vacation budget.

Being Sneaky – All passengers, including lapchildren, who are flying overseas will need to present a passport at airport check-in. If you think you can save a few dollars by saying your three-year-old is really only 22 months and just big for their age, you will be surprised by having to pay the price of a last-minute ticket if the rest of the family wants to proceed with their trip. With domestic flights, children do not necessarily need ID. This means boarding is up to the discretion of the gate attendant. If your child really is "big for their age," you may want to consider bringing a copy of their birth certificate along to avoid any potential hassles at check-in. Again, if you decide to try to pull a "fast one," bear in mind that you could be denied boarding altogether, or may have to pay a higher fare. Remember, airline safety rules are in place to keep both your child and all passengers safe.

Luggage – It's amazing how much "stuff" little humans need to be safe and comfortable. Most airplanes do not stock diapers, baby food or even offer changing facilities. It's recommended that parents pack a minimum one-day supply of these items, not to mention strollers, clothing, portable cribs, etc. Because you are not paying for an airline seat for lapchildren, this means you do not get any luggage allowance for them. This means mom and/or dad must pack all of junior's necessities into their carry-ons. Parents need to calculate the cost of excess or oversized luggage fees into the cost of their child's "free" ticket. You will need to do the "travel math" to calculate the savings of a free seat versus paying for luggage.

Size of Airline Seats – The average size of most airline seats is 14 by 16 inches with minimal legroom. Can you and your child sit comfortably in this size space for the length of your flight? Try out this test with a kitchen chair at home if you need any convincing. If it's a long flight, you won't be able to drop your tray table down for meals because there is simply no room. Also consider the feelings and comfort of fellow passengers seated around you. If they have paid full price for their ticket, they might not look kindly on a cranky child infringing on their space.

In Case of Emergency – Most airlines are outfitted with a limited number of oxygen masks per seat per row. With a lapchild, there may not be enough oxygen masks available.

COMPROMISES....

Time Your Flights – If possible try to schedule flights for travel times when airplanes are not full. Most folks prefer to fly early morning or after work. Parents with infants might prefer to fly during midafternoon naptime, which is when flights are generally less crowded. In addition, if flights are not full, airlines may offer parents with infants some options. They may allow parents to use their child's safety seat onboard and not pay for an extra ticket. The other option is they may seat parents next to empty seats to give lapchildren and their grownups a little extra space without the extra charge. Remember, this is a last-minute arrangement dependent on luck and totally up to the good graces of the airline and airport check-in staff. Parents can call 24 hours prior to departure and inquire about possibilities.

Fly Off-Season – Young families with non-school-age kids, or homeschoolers, can take advantage of huge vacation deals and discounts by traveling during early May, September, October or early December or January when other kids are in school. Compared to travel during summer vacation, holiday or spring break weeks, the cost difference can often pay for an airline seat for your baby.

Shop Around – Check nearby airports for both your departure and destination flights. Often by driving a little, parents can find good deals that can offset the cost of an additional ticket for your baby.

Your travel agent can always price a baby vacation for you with or without an airline seat for your baby. Fees, taxes and charges for lapchildren may not be listed in reservation systems so you or your travel agent may need to contact the airlines. Your agent may ask for the exact first, middle and last names of all passengers along with their dates of birth in order to put space on a courtesy hold. You are under no obligation, but often the airlines will not release lapchild charges until seats are on hold.

Just remember, airline ticket names must EXACTLY match ID or passport documents to avoid any penalties or change fees with the airlines. If you are flying outside of the country, your baby WILL need a valid passport. It generally takes four to six weeks to obtain a passport. You can go ahead and make reservations before applying for your child's passport. Just be certain that the first, middle and last name of your child's reservation matches their passport or passport application EXACTLY or you may find yourself paying name change fees.

Airport Security with a Baby

Nothing puts fear into the hearts of traveling parents like having to pass through airport security with a baby. The Transportation Safety Administration (TSA) is responsible for screening all passengers and their luggage at the airport prior to their flights. Yes, it's inconvenient to be pulling out our laptops and taking off our shoes, especially while trying to juggle little ones. It is important to remember that the TSA is there to keep us all safe. Help is available for parents; all you need to do is speak up and ask for assistance if you need it. Knowing what to expect and being prepared will certainly make inspection easier and less frightening for parents.

ID Requirements – Children under the age of 18 are not required to have an ID to fly on domestic flights within the United States. Babies, toddlers and all children flying internationally to foreign countries are required to have a valid US Passport.

Baby Carriers – Parents must carry infants through TSA security checkpoints. Infant carriers need to be put through X-ray screening machines. Nobody wants to disturb a sleeping child but sadly infant carriers have been used to hide explosives and other contraband.

You and Your Baby Will Never Get Separated – If for any reason you or your child requires additional screening you will both go together. You can request a private screening area or you can request to speak to a supervisor if you feel additional screening is uncalled for.

Baby Liquids – Parents are allowed to bring medications, baby formula and food, breast milk, and juice in reasonable quantities. These types of liquids are not governed by the 3.4 ounces (100ml) limit and do not have to be contained in a Ziploc bag (although Ziploc bags are a great idea for keeping your diaper bag contents dry and secure). Parents will need to make TSA agents aware that they are carrying extra liquids by declaring the need for a visual bag inspection. All other carry-on liquids like toothpaste, shampoo and deodorants must be in accordance with the TSA 3-1-1 rules. Google the specifics of these rules as they can change from time to time. Generally this means all other carry-on liquids must be in containers of three ounces or smaller and must fit into a quart size Ziploc bag. Only one bag is allowed per passenger.

Food and Snacks – Unless flying a very long flight, most airlines no longer serve meals. Most offer a very limited selection of snacks, which may not be the best, healthy choices. Parents should bring formula, snacks and meals onboard for both their babies and themselves. The best choices are pre-packaged foods. Fresh fruits and vegetables are often not allowed, especially when crossing international borders.

Many larger airports have special security lines for families and passengers who may need extra assistance. This often makes traveling parents with infants and toddlers a bit more relaxed. Being in line with fellow sympathetic parents is often more reassuring than delaying an anxious laptop-toting, slip-on shoe businessman.

Once you've had your initiation flight with your little one, you'll appreciate that it's often far less difficult in real life than it is in your imagination. No worries! You've got this!

Car Seats

As mentioned earlier, if you are purchasing an airline seat for your baby then you will absolutely need to bring your car seat along. You will also need to make sure it is an FAA approved seat suitable for airline use. If you choose not to buy an airline seat for your baby under 24 months, chances are you will still need to bring your car seat along for the ride.

All 50 states, the District of Columbia, Guam, the Northern Mariana Islands and the Virgin Islands require child safety seats for infants. If you're flying within the United States you'll install your car seat in your relative's ride or rental car just as though you would when driving the family car at home.

But what if your flight is taking you and your child overseas to a different country? Car seat laws can vary dramatically in foreign countries from what parents are familiar with back home in the states. Many countries do not require children to use any sort of car seat or safety restraint. For this reason, in foreign countries automobiles may not be equipped with anchors or seatbelt-locking retractors necessary to safely install US car seats.

Child seat anchor systems have been standard equipment in US and Canadian cars since 2002. In Europe, it's called ISOFIX and has been available since 2007.

So what's a parent to do? Here are some options to help you make the best decisions for your family:

1. Car safety seats are NOT required on public transportation, even here in the United States. If you choose to let your baby to fly as a lapchild and do not want to bring a car seat, you can elect to use public transportation to get to your hotel and for your sightseeing excursions.

2. Check with transportation or car rental companies at your foreign destination. They may offer car seat rentals for an additional fee. Bear in mind these car seats may or may not be equivalent to US safety standards. Ask if they have vehicles built to US standards that DO have latch systems for US car seat installation. You may be able to obtain this type of vehicle with a simple request. Many other car rental or transportation companies will require you to pay an upgrade fee for a vehicle with car seat latch features but it will solve your dilemma.

3. Contact the customer care department of your car seat manufacturer and ask for their recommendation. Some car seats come with a car seat clip that fits over the car's seat belt system to lock your car seat in place. If your car seat didn't come with this clip, you can purchase one for usually less than $10 online. This clip simply slides over the car's existing seat belt and will help anchor LATCH-system seats into older cars or those from other countries without proper anchors.

This way you'll always be prepared and ready for any unexpected situation while traveling and have the peace of mind knowing you've done your best to keep your little one safe, happy and sound.

Strollers

Chances are, if you're flying with a baby or toddler, you will need to bring a stroller.

Your first consideration should be your family vacation destination. Will your stroller help or hinder you? If your child is small enough, a baby carrier or backpack might be a much more efficient way to go. A stroller may not be practical for a beach vacation or fit very well in a family cruise cabin.

Many family friendly vacation spots have strollers for families to use. Some resorts offer these for free while others charge a small daily fee. You will definitely need a stroller for a Disney park vacation. You can rent strollers directly from guest services in the park or many other area vendors which you can search online.

"Stuff happens" while traveling. It's never a good idea to travel with anything really valuable. This advice holds true for bringing your stroller along on your trip. If you own an expensive, tricked out stroller, consider how you would feel if it were lost or damaged. For this reason, you may want to consider picking up a cheap umbrella stroller for your trip. If it's lost or stolen, you won't be heartbroken.

Another consideration may be how many strollers you need for the little ones in your family. If you are parents to multiples or stair-step kids, you may require more than a one-seat stroller. On my last trip to Disney I held the door for a family with three-year-old quadruplets wheeling a double-double-wide, four-seater stroller. If this sounds like your family, BE SURE to double-check with specific airline baggage rules. Some airlines have size restrictions and do not allow double-wide or oversize strollers. You may need to opt for multiple strollers.

Rest assured, you will be able to use your stroller to wheel your little ones through the airport. You will need to collapse it and put it through airport security X-ray machines. Parents must carry their little ones through the scanners. You will be able to use your stroller while waiting at the gate.

When the time comes to board your airplane, you will be allowed to wheel your stroller down the jetway. Right before you step onto the airplane, airline staff will be waiting to "gate check" your stroller. They will tag your stroller and give you a claim ticket with a number on it. Be sure to keep this safe until you are reunited with your stroller when you step off your aircraft at your destination. Airlines will NOT allow you to bring strollers onboard as a carry-on item.

Bear in mind, your stroller will be placed in underplane storage. These cargo holds are filthy, often wet and muddied. Many parents opt to use gate check stroller bags to help keep their strollers clean for their little ones. These bags can be easily purchased online and are a cheap insurance that your stroller will remain clean and protected for your baby. Make sure you have your name and cell phone number written on or tagged to both your stroller and stroller bag.

Choosing the Right Hotel

Some hotels and resorts are more baby-friendly than others. This is where the help of a travel agent can be invaluable. Choosing the right resort room that comes fully equipped with all the baby gear you will need will be far more comfortable and convenient for your family. It will also save on airline luggage fees for things like portable cribs and baby seats.

Just like with car seats, bear in mind that safety rules for baby equipment may be different or nonexistent in some foreign countries. Crib slats or even balcony railings could be a hazard. For this reason, some parents may prefer to pay the extra luggage fees and bring their own gear from home.

When traveling with an infant, location and convenience are the keys to your family's comfort and enjoyment. This is one of those situations where upgrading either your resort choice or room category is often a very smart decision. Many foreign hotels and resorts do not offer elevators. With older kids this may not be a problem but when traveling with an infant, it's important to request a ground floor room. Remember this is usually upon "request" and not guaranteed. Choosing a one-bedroom suite is often a smart upgrade that will help give parents an area to escape to after putting their little one down for the night. These units will often offer a refrigerator and at least a microwave, which will help during middle of the night feedings.

There are a few all-inclusive resorts that do offer baby care as a complimentary service for their guests. Most of these resorts are found in the Caribbean and Mexico. Usually these resorts have a separate nursery area complete with toys, cribs and baby gear that is open for certain hours every day. Each resort has specific rules and age requirements. Parents can "drop off" their babies for supervised care. Normally parents are given a "pager" or must leave their cell phone number. "Nursery staff will notify parents if their baby becomes fussy or needs attention.

If parents choose to use resort baby care facilities to care for their infants, parents must remain on resort property. This means Mom and Dad can go to the pool, the beach, eat in the restaurants or schedule an appointment at the spa. Parents are not allowed to leave the resort to play golf or go scuba diving or sightseeing. They must remain close by and available for their infants at all times.

Private babysitting is also available in most hotels. Nannies or private babysitters can be hired for an additional hourly fee. Normally these sitters are outside contractors and not hotel employees. Again every resort has different pricing and rules. Normally these arrangements need to be made with the concierge at least 24 hours in advance. Some hotels will allow private babysitters to care for infants in the parents' hotel room(s). Other resorts require all babysitting, even after-hours care, to be given in public areas like the nursery or kid's club for security reasons. In a few rare cases, parents can leave the resort but are required to hire a private nanny to care for their infants during their absence. Once again, this is one of those circumstances where your travel agent can help you make the best choices and give you all of your child-care options.

Some resorts may not offer free baby care or babysitting services but may offer playgroups for babies and toddlers. These are specific, scheduled times when parents can visit the kid's club with their babies and use the facilities for playtime. Parents must accompany and stay with their babies at all times. It's a fun time for your little one and a great way for parents to make friends and socialize with other moms and dads staying at the resort. Some resorts also offer "toy-lending" programs. Think of this like "borrowing" a library book. Parents can "borrow" toys for their little ones to play with while in their room or on the beach and simply return them when they are done playing.

Do know that the number of resorts that offer baby care is very limited. If free baby care sounds appealing on your next vacation, do your best to plan ahead. The hotels that do offer this program tend to sell out quickly. Parents appreciate this service and are often amazed at how few hotels offer baby care. To understand why, parents need to think like a hotel owner. It is far more profitable for hoteliers to allocate space for a spa. Paying guests will pay even more money for spa treatments and this adds additional revenue and profits to the hotel owner's bottom line. Adding baby care means a huge liability, additional insurance coverage and staff salaries all for the benefit of "non-paying" guests. Most resorts don't charge for babies, and for this reason do not see the point of adding services for free guests. Most parents would argue that baby care is a service that benefits hotel sales by enticing parents to stay and I would tend to agree.

Of course every parent will have differing opinions as to whether or not they feel comfortable leaving their baby in the care of others, whether in a resort or on a ship. This is an individual decision that each family must make for themselves. Also, some babies will adapt better than others to new caregivers and surroundings. Babies who normally spend time in a day care setting may have an easier time in a resort or ship nursery compared to those who spend their days with a stay-at-home mom or dad. Parents will need to assess the level of care offered and decide whether or not it meets their individual standards.

If parents aren't comfortable leaving their infant in the care of nursery staff then their option would be to travel with help or in the company of extended family. Whether parents bring others along to help care for baby is of course best discussed in the initial vacation planning stages. As we discussed earlier, it is often difficult to simply "add on" passengers to a reservation at the last minute. Additional people may not be allowed in the room or cabin due to occupancy rules. Adding a babysitter may make for a lack of privacy and awkward situation for everyone. Also hotel and airline rates nearly always increase as the time gets closer to departure. In many cases, traveling off season is a good compromise. The difference in pricing will make bringing a babysitter from home more affordable. This way parents can relax knowing that their little one is getting the best attention. Off-season rates can mean the difference between a standard room or a one-bedroom suite offering more space and privacy.

Dressing and Packing for Baby

New family vacations can be adventures in hot weather, cold weather and everything in between. Packing the appropriate items can mean the difference between a happy or cranky child.

Dress the part. Layers are a traveler's best friend, regardless of age. To keep a watch on the overall temperature of your baby, slip your fingers down the back of their neck or chest to check core body temperature. Also check to make sure fingers and toes are just right too.

If you're heading off on a tropical trip, a wide brimmed hat will keep the sun off delicate skin areas like ears and the back of the neck. Baby sunglasses will protect little eyes from UV rays while staying in place. Hot sand can hurt delicate baby feet, not to mention shells and stones. Sandals or flip-flops may look cute but do not provide the same protection as water shoes. Diaper bag secret: besides your normal bag of diaper changing tricks, did you know a little cornstarch can be used to rid body parts of pesky beach sand? Sprinkle it onto dry sandy feet and simply brush the sand off.

Infants younger than six months need to be kept in the shade, out of direct sunlight. Sometimes a lightweight camping tent can provide shade or act as a windbreaker. If you're worried about sunscreens, there is also the option of sun protective clothing and beach gear.

Remember, even though it can be really hot, air conditioning can change that the second you step indoors. You may want to pack a thin hoodie or hat for cool or breezy evenings for your little one. If you and your baby will be traveling in cooler weather, remember to pack mitts and extra socks along with winter covers.

If you'll be traveling in the winter, make sure you have a hat that covers your baby's ears. Use a jacket and blanket or bunting so that your baby will be warm while your car seat is doing its job. Delicate skin will be more sensitive to temperature changes, so be sure to moisturize. Opt for a sleep sack or "footie" pajamas. If it's really cold, and layers of onesies and socks underneath.

Swim Diapers

Vacationing with a child who is not yet potty trained comes with its own set of challenges. One planning issue parents need to keep in mind when selecting a resort or cruise ship is whether or not your child will be allowed to use the pool. Many pools specify health rules regarding the use of swim diapers. Often rules are determined by the age of a pool, the time of filtration system and local health ordinances.

Just in case you've been living in the dark ages, a swim diaper is a disposable diaper made from a special material that will supposedly absorb poop and pee but will not swell up with pool water while your baby or toddler is swimming. There are also specific covers made for parents using cloth diapers that are designed with the same purpose in mind.

According to the Centers for Disease Control and Prevention, any swim diaper offers a false sense of security because they can leak. Urine is not really the issue. It surprises many people to learn that urine from a healthy person is sterile and germ free. The problem is poop. Fecal material contains many germs that can cause illness... *E. coli*, *Giardia*, and particularly *Cryptosporidium*, which is a chlorine-resistant parasite that can cause diarrhea. If your baby or toddler enters a pool with a leaky, poopy diaper then your child and everyone using the pool is at risk to become sick.

Not all resorts or cruise lines or cruise ships will allow babies and toddlers in their main pools or especially hot tubs. Newer family-friendly resorts and cruise ships have been designed with specific baby pools. These pools are smaller in size with a separate, dedicated filtration system allowing for easy and effective sanitation. Splash parks offer babies and toddlers cool, wet fun. In a splash park, diapers are not totally submerged as they would be in a regular pool so it does somewhat help to prevent the spread of germs.

Even though you understand the health importance of these issues and abide by the rules, unfortunately the same isn't true for everyone. Cultural and language differences may mean that your family will encounter other families that allow their babies to swim with regular diapers or even naked. The cruise lines do an excellent job of supervising and enforcing their rules, but challenges may occur. So how do you enjoy your own family vacation time while protecting your family's health and safety? Here are a few tips...

- If you are not sure about hotel or cruise ship rules on swim diapers, be sure to ASK first and never assume that it is okay.

- Work with a travel agent who specializes in family vacations to help you find the best baby- or toddler-friendly ship for your family cruise.

- Supervise your child at all times while swimming.

- If your child is allowed to use swim diapers be sure to check frequently to see if a change is necessary.

- Change any diapers in a designated bathroom area and not poolside as this can also facilitate the spread of germs.

- Use proper handwashing techniques after all diaper changes.

- Discourage children from taking any pool water into their mouths.

If your baby or toddler shows any signs of diarrhea or illness, especially while on vacation, keep them far away from any public pool areas until you can visit a doctor.

Please bear in mind that there may be other vacationing families sharing facilities who may be dealing with health and safety issues like chronic medical conditions, a suppressed immune system or even pregnancy. Your child's swim diaper could create a life-threatening situation for them.

If the idea of public swimming areas and swim diapers simply grosses you out, one option is to bring along a small, inflatable swimming pool for your little one on your next vacation. This way your baby can splash and stay cool while you enjoy a bit more peace of mind. You'll need to ask how to properly dispose of the water from your inflatable pool when you're finished to maintain ship health and safety standards. An inflatable pool can also double as a bathtub in some cruise ship cabins that do not offer a bathtub.

Sun Protection

Depending on your choice of destination, sun protection can be a significant concern. It's always best to get your pediatrician's advice. The American Academy of Dermatology recommends that children over six months of age use a broad-spectrum sunscreen with an SPF of at least 30. Parents need to apply sunscreen generously and be sure to apply at least every two hours, especially after spending time in the water. Set the alarm on your phone to remind you to reapply. Sun protective clothing choices will also help, especially hats.

If you plan to spend the day at the beach or by the pool, umbrellas and shade coverings for portable cribs can help beyond the branches of a swaying palm tree. Many parent will carry small pop up tents as a means of portable shade no matter where they roam.

The hot rays of the sun can also lead to dehydration, especially for young children. Speak with your pediatrician regarding their advice for supplementing formula or nursing with additional fluids.

TRAVELING WITH TODDLERS (AGES 2–4)

Many of the travel tips offered in this book (see the chapter "Vacationing with Baby") will also apply when it comes to traveling with toddlers. Tots between two to four years of age will still need a stroller for long distances. They will still need appropriate car-safety seats. Depending on their ages and abilities, much of the information in the baby section will still be important.

But once your child becomes mobile it's a whole new world of parenting! Safety becomes a major issue when vacationing with a toddler. Parents may have their home childproofed, but being away from home requires extra diligence. Toddlers are quick and require extra vigilance in crowded airports, theme parks and pools. Parents need extra eyes and hands on deck at all times so it's a great time for vacationing with grandparents, extended family or friends. Having extra help means parents may have some very well-deserved "me" time to relax and chill.

Toddlers over the age of two will require their own airline seat for all flights. Cruise lines also charge by the number of passengers sharing a cabin regardless of age. That said, toddlers can score some great travel deals for their families. Many all-inclusive resorts allow children under the age of five to "stay, play and eat" free. Find a resort that offers free child care for toddlers and it's a great deal for parents. Many hotels that have a maximum occupancy rate of four will often allow a toddler as a fifth guest in that room. This can be a huge budget saver for families of five.

Parents of toddlers are not yet tied to a school calendar. This means that, when everyone else's kid is in school, you can usually score big savings, especially during off-season times like September. This can mean overall savings of 40–70% for the entire family.

The biggest mistakes parents of toddlers make when planning vacations is time management. Toddlers simply require more time to do everything than other humans. Whether this means napping, dressing, eating or sightseeing—time is of the essence. Just because Mom and Dad have done a particular road trip many times in just one day doesn't mean they will be able to expect a repeat performance with their two-year-old in tow. Add in naptime, mealtime, bathroom time, distraction time, playtime, silly time, and discovery time to the itinerary, and you can see that it will take the family twice as long to cover the same amount territory. New compromises will need to be made—like parental "shift sleeping"—so that most of the driving can be done at night while your little one is dreaming away in the car seat. Allowing an extra day upon arrival to rest up before diving into all of your planned vacation fun could certainly translate into a more enjoyable plan for all.

Tolerable travel with a toddler has a lot to do with practicality. It could also mean extra travel costs like upgrading your hotel to a much more convenient location close to the theme park so it's easy to pop back for a nap or "costume change." These upgrades do not need to break the bank if you plan your itinerary accordingly with these creature comfort compromises in mind from the start. Using off-season rates to your advantage, and making smart splurges with vacation spending will certainly give you the most bang for your vacation buck.

Potty training is another compromise to consider when planning a vacation with a toddler. Swim diapers were previously discussed in our baby chapter. Besides the concerns about packing or acquisition of supplies, many pools, resort and cruise kid's clubs have strict health and safety rules in place for toddlers who wear diapers. Parents may decide to time their vacation accordingly, or opt for one type of accommodation over another depending on how accomplished your toddler is with the potty.

It is really important to try to keep toddlers on their daily routines and schedules as much as possible while not overloading the family's vacation itinerary. That said, travel can wreak havoc on a toddler's routine. For this reason, parents should not expect perfection. The type of vacation or tour that requires the timing of military precision should be left until your child is older and better equipped. Parents taking a toddler on vacation need to recognize that the best made plans are the plans that are often broken or changed. Flexibility is the key to success. The expectation of perfection will lead to stress and disappointment. Instead, embracing the joy of serendipity and living in the moment can produce a lifetime of memories for the family to enjoy.

Parents are often delighted and surprised by how much toddlers grasp and how quickly they learn new things. Be sure that you include your toddler in your vacation planning. Using age-appropriate picture books and bedtime stories can be a great way to introduce your child to the idea of visiting a new place, traveling by boat or sleeping in a new bed. Take the time to explain as much as you possibly can to prepare your child for the exciting things everyone will get to see and do on your family vacation.

Remind yourself to think like a child. Often children will have concerns that they may not be able to easily communicate or verbalize. For example, be sure to explain that you are only leaving home for a few days. Make it a counting game. Let your child know that you will all be returning home to normal life and that you won't be staying on vacation forever. They will soon be home again surrounded by all their favorite people and toys, and sleeping in their own bed. Other concerns children may have might be leaving grandparents and friends, or even worries about who will be caring for their pets. Do your best to have age-appropriate conversations ready and try to alleviate any fears your child will have about traveling.

Try to include your child as much as possible in your travel preparations. Countdown calendars are a fun way to give your child a sense of when your big travel day will come. Packing can be turned into a fun game of "this or that to pack." Give your child two choices and let them make the final decision of what goes into the suitcase. Any age-appropriate ideas and tricks to help engage your little one with your travel preparations will help to keep them cooperative.

As parents, do your best not to appear nervous or stressed. Your child will sense your anxiety, which could lead to meltdowns. Give your child a proper example to follow.

Flying with Toddlers

Toddlers love nothing better than to explore the world around them, so use this to your advantage when traveling. If you are planning to take a flight with your toddler, plan an airport "practice run." Plan a visit to the airport on a day when you're not flying anywhere. Let your child take in all the people, sights and sounds. Give them plenty of time to simply explore. Spend time watching the airplanes. Explain how airport security works. Have a lunch, do a little shopping and make it a fun day. This way, on the day of departure, your child will be experienced with the airport sights, sounds and experiences, and be familiar with the entire experience.

Make sure to give yourself plenty of extra time when trying to accomplish any travel task with your toddler. When possible, be sure to do online checks and get your family's boarding passes 24 hours prior to your departure. This will save you and your toddler time waiting in line at the airport. Plan your ride to the airport in advance or schedule a parking reservation ahead of time to save time. If airport check-in time is one hour prior to departure for domestic US flights and two hours for international flights, add an extra hour for toddler time. Many parents may think this suggestion is counterintuitive. But having time to play at an airport playground or have fun watching the planes instead of feeling rushed and stress can work to your advantage.

Dealing with TSA security checks can be very stressful for some children. Again, explain to your child ahead of time what they can expect so that the experience will be less scary. Let your child know that they will be required to get out of their stroller and walk with you through the X-ray machines. Tell your child that the X-ray machine will not hurt or be painful in any way. Do let your child know that they will need to part with their favorite toy or blanket while it passes through security. A good way to present this idea is to ask your child to sing their favorite song once or twice. By the time they are finished singing, they will be reunited with their beloved item. If you do a practice airport visit and if you can visualize the airport X-ray machines, play a counting game – each time a traveler puts their items on the conveyor, make a prediction and count how long it takes to pass through to be collected on the other side – one Mississippi, two Mississippi, etc. On the day of travel, have your child play the counting game and see how long it takes until they get their item back.

Toddlers in Hotels

As your child begins to crawl, walk and explore, parents quickly begin to barricade and lock up their homes. It becomes a serious matter of safety. Electric sockets, wires and blind pulls all need attention. Windows and doors need to be locked and secured. Suddenly the entire world becomes a huge safety hazard.

Vacations are meant to be a fun escape from reality but when traveling with a toddler, responsibility travels with you. At home, you might be the poster parents as far as safety is concerned, and you need to pack this awareness with you when you travel with your toddler.

Many hotels and resorts will offer "childproofing" for toddlers. This may include kits complete with wall socket plugs and extra latches. Upon arrival, parents should get down on their hands and knees in order to explore their new room directly from their child's eye view. Ask hotel staff to remove any fixtures with dangling cords or furniture that could pose a climbing hazard. If your sliding door doesn't have a high lock, ask for an additional security bar to be placed in the door track. Another important point parents need to watch for are poisoning hazards. Often, parents will pack toiletries and medications in different containers to comply with airport security. These containers may not be childproof and could be dangerous if found by an inquisitive toddler. Safety concerns are also important if you are traveling with, or even visiting, grandparents or extended family members who are not used to keeping medications or other hazards in childproof containers.

As toddlers grow so do other safety concerns. If your child became separated from you in an airport, would they know who to ask for help? If a stranger knocked on your hotel door, would they know how to react? If a family member needed emergency medical help would your child know what to do?

Of course, vacations are meant to be fun and carefree, but bad things can happen to good people at any place and at any time. Travel and vacation time offers parents the opportunity to teach and review safety training with our kids. Parents can set the example for kids demonstrating that personal safety deserves our attention and respect. Simple things like being respectful during airline safety demos, learning how to dial a hotel phone for help, or making sure they memorize your cell phone number as soon as they are able, are all little things you can do to help them help themselves should a crisis occur.

Of course we want to keep our kids safe without making them fearful. Still, at this age parents and kids need all the help they can get. Some parents may want to go high-tech with GPS tracking devices when taking their kids into crowded places on vacation. Disney World now offers guests staying in the park at a Disney Resort "Magic Bands" to wear on their wrists. Technically these bracelets are used as your room keys, park passes, restaurant reservations and fast pass info. They also offer Disney cast members easier ways to reunite parents with lost children. One quick scan of the kids' wrist will link to the parent's reservation, which usually contains their cell phone number. Some of the newer cruise ships offer similar technology. Kids wear a bracelet with a GPS chip when off at the kid's club. Parents can go to any informational computer onboard and see exactly whether their child is in the club or at the pool or buffet with staff. Of course there are also low-tech safety options for parents traveling with kids. Items like backpack leashes or safety tattoos are available. Parents will have differing opinions about the use of these and other tools that are available for keeping kids safe. Give yourself time prior to your trip to do a little homework, discuss and decide what will work best for your kids.

In addition, your hotel may be able to provide comfort features like a stepstool for the bathroom sink or potty-seat. Luxury family resorts will even offer slippers, miniature robes and bath amenities (including rubber ducks) geared specifically for toddlers. There may even be nighttime turndown service with chocolates or cookies so be alert if you don't want your child snacking at bedtime.

Most hotels and resorts will provide either a crib or a cot. If your toddler is too big for a crib and may fall during their sleep from a cot, ask if the hotel provides bedrails. If not, removing the cot mattress to the floor or using an air mattress may be a safer alternative. If there is a couch in your room, another alternative is to turn the couch around to face the wall. This may provide your toddler with a more secure sleeping area. For little-sized humans, another great alternative is an inflatable raft or air mattress. Depending on exactly what you choose, it can double as a pool toy as well as a safe sleeping area with no fear of bedtime falls.

Just like nursery care, resort child care for toddlers is in short supply and for the very same reasons. There are a few more hotels and all-inclusive resorts that do allow toddlers into their free child care programs. Still, toddler care programs are in short supply and resorts that do offer this service generally do sell out early, especially during busy travel times.

Usually the one qualifying caveat is that your toddler must be fully potty trained to be able to participate in most toddler care programs. Due to health regulations in many locations, child care staff in these programs will not change diapers. Ask your travel professional for help and guidance to find a resort and program suited to the needs of your family.

As mentioned earlier with the nursery programs, if your toddler does participate in these complimentary resort toddler programs, parents are not allowed to leave the resort property for excursions. At least one parent must be present on resort property at all times. Once again, every hotel does have its own rules governing individual or in-room private babysitting. Generally this needs to be arranged 24 hours in advance with the concierge department.

Cruising with a Toddler

Finding a fun cruise vacation to take with your toddler simply means a bit of matchmaking. It's about finding the right balance of comfort and activity. Cruise vacations are great because your family can travel great distances while your little one is asleep so that you can cover a great deal of territory. Family-friendly cruises now sail to just about every port on the globe, so there are plenty of exciting choices of destinations. All of your food and shipboard entertaining is easily accessible and included in the price of your cabin. Speaking of dining, there are plenty of options from quick buffets to room service and evening babysitting so that mom and dad can enjoy a romantic meal together.

By this age, you'll probably already know if your child has any sensitivity to motion sickness. If your child has tummy troubles on car rides then there is a good chance they may have seasickness issues onboard a cruise ship. As always, seek the input of your pediatrician who can offer the best medical advice specific to your toddler's health.

The good news is that most children normally outgrow this problem. A few of us, including myself, continue to be sensitive to motion sickness well into adulthood. The latest good news is that many of the newer ships have been built with state of the art stabilization systems. New technology helps to ensure smoother sailing. I speak from personal experiences as a reluctant cruiser when I say that my last few cruises on the newer mega ships were fun and completely free of dizziness or any stomach issues.

If you still remain concerned about how your little one will tolerate the water, try a test run. If possible plan a "practice day" out on a lake or local beach with a short boat ride. If your child tolerates that without incident, chances are they will become a fine sailor. If you're still feeling a little insecure, try booking your family for a few days at the beach along with a shorter cruise of two to three nights to test the waters.

Choosing the right cabin when you are cruising with a toddler can mean all the difference between success and failure. Just because your cruise cabin will fit three or more family members doesn't mean it will be configured for your comfort. Most double cruise ship cabins come with two convertible twin beds that can be separated or joined together depending on the preferred sleeping arrangements of the two people sharing that cabin. Many of the cheaper triple or quad cabins that allow three or four people to share a cabin have "uppers" or "upper berths." These are high bunk beds that pull out of the wall. Upper berths are very practical for saving floor space but totally impractical when cruising with a toddler. Consider opting for a different style cabin, with either a foldout sofa or enough floor space for an inflatable or regular cot mattress.

Some cruise lines are a bit more toddler-friendly than others. Each one has specific rules as to what age toddlers can participate in their free child care in their kid's club programs.

Toddlers in Theme Parks

Toddler time is often the first time many parents will select a theme park vacation. This is the age when kids start recognizing specific characters and do have a great deal of wonder and imagination. Speaking of great deals, usually kids under the age of three enjoy free admission to Disney Parks and others. Depending on your family and length of stay, this would save parents a few hundred dollars if they time their vacation before the clock strikes midnight on their toddler's third birthday.

Theme parks offer a lot of stimulation for little ones with short attention spans. There are plenty of attractions, characters and even animals that are sure to capture your child's curiosity. It's also a place that is full of parents and kids so no worries or embarrassment if your child has an unexpected meltdown.

The trick to enjoy a theme park with your toddler is to avoid meltdowns whenever possible. Here are three "don'ts" to keep in mind:

1. **Don't skimp on a hotel room** – When traveling with a toddler it is all about "location, location, location." This is the time to upgrade to a deluxe hotel that is located as close to the park as possible and will allow you to conveniently take a break back at the hotel for a nap, a dip in the pool or a quick costume change if need be. If your child is not yet school-age, take advantage of low-season rates and travel in September when all the other kids are back at school. The cost difference will help with your hotel upgrade and make for a much more enjoyable time for the entire family.

2. **Don't overload** – Of course you want to get as much vacation bang for your buck but do not be tempted to cram your daily itinerary. Toddlers operate on their own schedules, so do plan for serendipitous moments. Often these are the ones you'll remember for years to come. You will cover more ground with less aggravation if you plan for frequent stops, time-outs for play and naps.

3. **Don't force the issue** – You may have your heart set on a photo op with your child's favorite character but your child may have other ideas. If your child is frightened of getting up close with a character or is afraid of a particular attraction don't press the issue.

What if you have other kids in tow or perhaps this is a first time park visit for Mom and Dad who also have certain "must do's" on their vacation wish lists – how do you manage? Just about every major theme park offers a rider's switch. The family can wait in line once, one parent enjoys the ride while the other parent supervises and waits with the child. When the first parent is done riding then they switch. With newer attractions, these child swap areas are becoming more interactive and immersive play areas.

The tricky bit when planning a family vacation with a toddler is to find a balance. Parenting a toddler is an overtime job in addition to your day job. Moms and dads deserve a bit of "me" time too. Giving yourself some time to relax and recharge will indeed help you to be an even better parent. Schedule a babysitter to give yourself time to do something just for you. This may be a good time to travel as a tribe. Bring extended family members with you who can lend a helping hand. Travel with trusted friends who have kids similar in age and plan for some "trade-off time". This way it affords both families a little bit of balance.

It is true, no matter where you go with a toddler, it can be a challenge. Some parents may think it's best to wait and not take a vacation until their child is a bit older and a little more "civilized." Travel is a learned behavior. In the same way we teach our kids how to brush their teeth or tie their shoes, we need to teach them how to behave on a plane or how to behave mannerly in a restaurant.

Many parents worry about looks and comments from others when traveling with a toddler. Do not let this put you off your game. Remember, everyone was a toddler at one time or another. If you feel your child's behavior may be a problem to fellow passengers, having a couple of $5 Starbucks gift cards in your pocket is a great way to apologize. If your child acts like an angel then you can look forward to a caffeine boost on your vacation.

SCHOOL-AGE KIDS (AGES 5–10)

In my humble opinion, these years are the "sweet spot" for family vacations. Children can pretty much care for their own personal needs. Learning, curiosity and imagination are at an all-time high. Best of all, they are not embarrassed to be seen in public with their parents. Instead they crave and appreciate your attention so get it while you can, moms and dads!

This is the age where parents can really have fun with their kids. Children are tall enough to go on many theme park attractions. They have the understanding and tolerance for longer flights. They meet the age requirements for many more adventure activities and sports. School age is when many kids qualify to vacation with their parents on escorted or guided tours. There will be more information on this in later chapters but know that it opens up yet another world of travel opportunities for your family.

This is the age when your children will develop their own passions and their own interests. Kids this age can tell you every factoid about fighter planes, know the living habits of every dinosaur or recite complicated rap lyrics without taking a breath. They are involved with all sorts of new and exciting activities and crave even more.

Of course, the best way to engage kids of this age is to feed into their passions and, when possible, expand upon them. Family vacations are a fantastic tool for expanding the horizons of your child and the entire family.

Most vacation itineraries can be created and customized around just about anything that your child is passionate about. Some may be obvious like a visit to the Smithsonian's National Air and Space Museum, astronaut camp, or NASA for the fighter jet fan. There are even experiences like camps where you dig for fossils alongside archeologists, and resorts with recording studios and DJ schools.

Naturally parents of this age group want to cultivate learning. Lack of funding has forced many schools to curtail art and music programs. While parents understand the necessity for this type of creative learning it may be something that their child hasn't really been exposed to at school. Vacation time may seem like the perfect time to kill two birds with one stone. Problems come when learning is forced. Wandering aimlessly around an art museum to give your kid "some culture" may not be a good way to do it. Meet your kids in the middle with a museum art camp day. Engage them with a "meet and greet" event with their favorite cartoon artist and build from there. To keep kids focused and engaged, it needs to be a balance of "info-tainment" – a fun experience where learning is the side effect.

The good news here is that now that your kids are learning to read, do math and make calculated decisions they can become more involved in the entire vacation planning process. Remember, when we talk about using family vacations as a means of education or info-tainment for our kids, it's not just about the destination, it's also about the journey.

Proper travel planning is a collection of wonderful life skills that would benefit any child – proper research, organization, budgeting, scheduling, problem solving, logistics, time management, etc. Involving kids in the vacation planning process empowers them and keeps them engaged throughout the trip.

I'm not suggesting that we hand over the reins and turn kids into travel agents. Give them some guidelines and let them be in control of some of the decision-making when appropriate. "On Wednesday, we're going to do a day trip. Should we all go horseback riding or snorkeling? Which would you choose?" Make a treasure hunt game for packing their suitcase. Give them a list – three pairs of pants, three shirts, etc., and let them decide on their favorites. Parents know chores like packing get done faster if we do them ourselves but taking a few extra minutes to involve kids pays long-term dividends.

Generally, school age is a busy time in the life of a family. Our kids keep us on the move with lots of extracurricular activities – sports teams, scouts, music and dance. It's often hard to get everyone on the same calendar page in order to take a vacation.

Sometimes this can mean some compromises. It may work better for your family's schedule to take a few weekend escapes instead of a full week adventure. This idea may also work if say one child has a particular passion that will drive other family members crazy. If your son and husband love to go camping and fishing, while the idea of spending time in the woods with bugs and poison ivy is not your idea of a good time, let them go. There is nothing carved in stone that says all family members have to travel together all the time and remain joined at the hip. Often the separation brings families closer together.

School-age kids are often faced with many different pressures like grades, homework deadlines and chores. Then there is the eternal struggle to find one's place in the world, to fit in and make friends. If your child isn't the round peg in the round hole they could be facing daily peer pressure, bullying and loneliness. Often we parents are the last to learn how difficult life can be for our kids.

Vacations offer kids the opportunity to meet others and make friendships beyond local neighborhood kids. For kids who have social troubles at home this can be a huge step to help them build confidence and self-esteem. My youngest was in special ed and was constantly bullied at school and on the bus. While on vacation, it doesn't matter which classroom is your homeroom or how good your grades are. Our family vacations allowed her to connect with other kids in a whole new way. She was able to create lasting friendships that have grown up with her over the years. Vacations help children gain a new perspective. It helps them to understand there is a great big world out there, far beyond the mean kids at school.

All of us, including children, NEED time to relax, unwind and simply have fun. Vacation is a time to escape our daily responsibilities. Kids need this as much as adults. Vacation time should be about fun. As parents we can take a vacation with our kids, but we can never take a vacation from BEING a parent. Of course, every family will need to make or break their own rules, but in the scheme of the universe, having chocolate cake for breakfast or a midnight bedtime while away on vacation won't be the end of the world.

Family Vacations and the School Calendar

Of course, the moment your kindergartener waves goodbye on their first day of school, vacation planning for your family changes dramatically. If you're like most families this means for the next 12–16 years that your travel plans will be tied to a school calendar.

This is a hot topic for many families and there can be a heated difference of opinions even within the same household. Personally I believe experience is the best teacher, and firsthand knowledge beats any book in the world. My personal opinion differed greatly from that of my local school board. I cannot begin to tell you the red tape, hassle and signed paperwork involved to take my own children out of school for a few days without fear of being placed on a watch list for child endangerment. Before taking your kids out of school to travel, be sure you fully understand the rules of your school and district.

Chances are that every child in your family learns differently. My oldest son was a very advanced learner and was bored in school. My middle daughter was that round peg in the round hole, got straight B's and was very flexible. My youngest daughter has severe dyslexia with short-term memory issues. School for her was a monumental challenge, so missing one day meant falling far behind. When deciding whether to take your kids out of school, parents must consider how the absence will affect their children's grades and stress levels.

Being tied to a school calendar means parents can expect to pay more for their family vacations. As mentioned earlier, the travel industry is all about supply and demand. When kids are out of school – holidays, spring break and summer vacation, rates for airlines, hotels and cruises go up. This also means availability becomes an issue. Parents simply cannot wait until the last minute to plan and book their trips. Again, we talked before about "planning your family vacation nine months in advance," but here are some more ballpark travel planning times for parents with school-age kids who are NOT flexible with travel dates...

- Disney theme parks – rates and availability are usually published midsummer for the following year, so start planning about 500 days in advance.

- Cruise lines – about 1.5 years in advance

- Resorts – about one year in advance up until early December, then December holiday rates about nine months in advance

- Guided tours – nine months to one year in advance

- Airlines – about nine months in advance. Parks, resorts and cruises should be booked as soon as their rates become available. Flights can always be added to your reservation. It is best to book flights as soon as they become available.

Often, parents with school-age kids may also need to juggle the needs of younger siblings. Preferred family-travel products like resorts with infant care, suites or cruise ship cabins for larger families, as well as guaranteed adjoining rooms are ALWAYS the first to sell out. Rates are at their lowest when they are first published and will climb as inventory sells. Flights especially will increase in price the closer it gets to departure. To avoid disappointment, parents must plan and make reservations in advance.

If you have a fear of commitment and booking your vacation that far in advance, know that many hotels, tours and cruises do offer flexible cancellation policies. If not, your vacation investment can be covered with travel insurance. Due to high demand during school holidays there is a very slim chance that any sales, perks or lower prices will become available but just in case, your travel agent can often get these prices adjusted, and there is also price-protection insurance.

Sometimes there are ways to "squeak" a good travel deal, even if your big breaks are governed by the school calendar. Some local school districts celebrate local "holidays" or schedule teacher's in-service days. For example, where we live, in Pennsylvania, the Monday following Thanksgiving is the opening day of the deer hunting season. Because deer hunting is such a family tradition in this area, many kids cut school that day to go hunting with their fathers and grandfathers. The school district finally caved and made it an "official" holiday. Of course, domestic flights and hotel rates take a jump as families gather for Thanksgiving. We found that if we left for a tourist destination like Cancun (where Thanksgiving isn't celebrated) on Friday, and returned late Monday night, we could squeak in a decent vacation at a good price.

Yes, early school-age years are the sweet spot for family vacations. As mentioned, it is also a hectic time with so many responsibilities competing for our time. It's easy to procrastinate or even say, "Our family is WAY too busy to even think about taking a vacation this year." Remember, this is often the age when parents can have the greatest impact on their children. It is also the time when kids can be the most fun, but it is only available for a very "limited engagement." Don't miss the boat!

TWEENS (AGES 10–12)

Tweens are just like the delicious frosting in the middle of an Oreo cookie. You have to break through the crunchy outside to get to the best part. Your kids are not babies anymore. Their friends are often held in higher authority than parents.

On one hand, tweens are optimistic creatures full of hopes, dreams and aspirations for the future. On the other, their preadolescent hormones are beginning to kick in. Tween girls are often described as "too old for toys and too young for boys." It's a tricky time for parents when their kids have outgrown some activities but aren't really old enough to or don't want to hang with adults.

Social Balance

Kids this age are very social creatures. Generally, their priority is to connect with their peers over having to spend time with their family. Tweens may resist the idea of taking a vacation with their families because it would mean their absence from their usual social circles. To them, a week away from home and their friends feels like a lifetime.

Planning the type of family vacation that offers some supervised independence and socialization opportunities for tweens often keeps everyone in harmony. Most of the cruise lines that cater to families do an excellent job with their kid's clubs or camps at sea. There are plenty of supervised, age-appropriate, scheduled activities throughout the day and even dancing, video game tournaments and entertainment in the evenings. The kid's clubs onboard cruise ships tend to break out tweens by age with more specific activities just for them. There are a few resorts that also cater specifically to this age group, but most simply offer group activities for kids say four to twelve years of age.

WiFi or Unplugged Family Vacations

Tweens are tech babies. Computers, video games, cell phones and tablets are as natural to them as breathing. They cannot imagine a world without them. They are usually more comfortable in the virtual world than they are in the real one.

This is another topic where parents are divided. Many parents crave a vacation with their teens where the kids are forced to "unplug" and reconnect with family members. "Someplace with limited WiFi service" is a trendy new family destination that is becoming ever more popular. In our travel agency we get this type of request often.

Other parents argue that, to keep their tweens interested and engaged on vacation, they MUST stay connected while away from home. Free WiFi service, ship-to-shore data plans, international cell service and free long-distance calling are amenities high on their family vacation wish lists.

No matter where parents stand on tech usage during family vacation time, it's a good idea to include these and a few other tween rules as you plan your family vacation. Discussing "rules of engagement" for vacations in advance is always best. Parents need to discuss and decide upon appropriate, acceptable behaviors and consequences for their tweens and make sure these rules are understood before ever leaving home. Tweens crave independence but they need to learn that this privilege must be earned and also comes with more responsibility.

Independence and Safety

Safety concerns for parents grow right along with kids. We don't want to frighten our children but we need to ensure their well-being. All of us want vacations that are fun, happy and carefree. No parent, or tween for that matter, wants to get into a heated argument about rules and curfews in paradise. Laying the groundwork for acceptable behavior before leaving home can help to prevent such conflicts.

Incentives and contracts can actually work wonders with tweens. Some may call it bribery. Others call it rewards for good behavior. Create a written contract outlining rules and expected behavior for the vacation, and if these rules are honored, your tween will have earned... a spa treatment or surfing lesson on the last day of the trip, be allowed to do XYZ when they get home, etc. This is an opportunity to teach tweens some more valuable life skills like contract law, responsibility, ownership and even the fine art of negotiation. It can also save parents a ton of debates and headaches.

TEENS (AGES 13–18)

Vacation budgets become matters of concern for many families. Once your child turns 13, they are considered full-fledged, paying adults by many in the travel industry. Not only does this affect the price your family pays but it also affects occupancy rules. For example, last year your hotel room may allow two adults and two kids under the age of 12. Once your child turns 13, that same hotel room may not allow your family of three adults and one child to share the same space.

By the age of 13, your teen has also outgrown many of the "kid's programs" offered at hotels and resorts. Resorts that do offer activity programs for teens tend to be pricier in order to pay for the costs of these extra programs. Most resorts with teen programs tend to lump teens into one large group despite the difference in maturity levels. You may not want your 13-year-old daughter hanging out in a late night teen disco with 18-year-old boys.

Cruise vacations offer many features that can really benefit families with teenagers. One of the biggest areas of benefit is their occupancy rules. Most family-friendly cruise lines charge by the number of guests sharing the same cabin regardless of their age. This means if yours is a family of four with a 16- and 14-year-old, Mom and Dad pay first and second passenger rates and the teens would pay much lower third or fourth passenger rates. If Mom and Dad prefer their privacy or don't want to share one bathroom, they can get guaranteed adjoining cabins. Everyone would pay the same "adult" rate but cruise ships allow you to choose your exact cabin. Adjoining hotel rooms are on a request basis only unless you pay for a specific category suite.

Besides the cabin benefits, the family cruise lines offer far more in the way of supervised activities for teens. Most separate these programs according to specific ages so as not to mix younger teens with older ones.

As teens get older, parents will find themselves using weekends or some of their vacation time to visit potential colleges. Obviously academics and living arrangements are the highest priorities for these types of trips. Still, if possible, give your family a little extra time to explore the local area. Your teen will not stay confined to the campus while at college. The local area, people and attractions will also affect their lifestyle in their new home away from home. The more accustomed your teens are to their new neighborhood, the easier it will be for them (and you) to adjust.

Drinking Laws

As always, safety is a parent's utmost concern when traveling with kids. Of course as kids grow, they encounter more "adult" problems. It is important to remember if you are traveling overseas with teens, different countries have different rules and regulations as far as legal age and drinking laws are concerned. Some countries will allow kids to drink at ages 16, 17, 18 and some have no laws at all for alcohol consumption.

Once again, each and every family has its own views regarding drinking and teens. Some parents believe abstinence is best while others believe drinking is okay if it is done under their supervision. Regardless of your point of view, it is important to be aware that the rules for drinking may be different when you are away from home. Once again, this is a situation that needs to be addressed, and rules put into place, before anyone steps with one foot out the door, in order to avoid arguments and chaos far from home. Teens need to understand that often, if they are allowed to drink like an adult, then legally they are as responsible as adults. This includes any and all consequences. Nobody wants that kind of vacation so it is best to avoid this situation by having all the facts.

Meals

Teenage boys are all about food. Most can easily consume the contents of an entire family refrigerator as a snack, turn around and call for pizza delivery. An average adult will spend about $50 per day on food and snacks while on vacation. Teenage boys can easily eat their way through twice that amount. Families with growing boys should really consider a vacation option that includes food, like an all-inclusive resort or cruise. If you are considering a theme park vacation then I would highly recommend adding a meal plan to help your budget. Having some sort of a meal plan will certainly help. The other option would be booking some sort of accommodation that offers a kitchen or cooking facilities like a condo, rental home or villa.

Packing

Seriously trying not to stereotype here but many teen girls can be "fashionistas." Often girls may to pack every outfit they own along with a truckload of cosmetics, shoes and accessories. Boys may toss their bathing suit, shorts, and some t-shirts along with one pair of socks and underwear into a bag and call it a day. Teens should be made responsible to pack their own bags. That said, they still may need some guidance.

Internet research is often a great task to delegate to teens. Have them research any evening dress codes for cruise ships or resort restaurants. Give them the task of researching luggage sizes and weight requirements before being surprised at airport check-in. Making them responsible for paying any oversize or overweight luggage fees often puts packing into perspective for them. Use the bathroom scale to double-check the weight on any bags you pack.

Bear in mind that many foreign hotels do not have elevators. Another way to curtail excess baggage is to give your teens a physical challenge. See if they can carry their own bags up and down three flights of stairs. Often this test results in much lighter luggage and is a great lesson in learning to set priorities.

Traveling without Family

Besides family vacations, this is also the age where teens may start traveling on their own. Traveling sports teams, band competitions, college inspections and school trips might be on your child's calendar. Hopefully by now if you have taken the advice of this book, your child is a road-savvy traveler and will know all the right things to do while traveling so they can avoid potential problems.

 If your teen is a novice traveler, do not assume that organizers and chaperones have done their jobs. Do YOUR homework, research the destination, itinerary, liability, accommodations, etc. Informed parents can help to create informed, safe and well-behaved teens. Bear in mind that your teen may require additional documentation and legal permissions when traveling in the company of others.

The "Last" Family Vacation

Earlier in this book I mentioned that parents only have a few short years to enjoy family vacations with their kids. Normally, when teens move out on their own or head off to college, the family dynamics change dramatically. This is not to say parents will never again vacation with their adult children – it's just "different."

For this reason, the "last family vacation" is a very important one. It's that the family vacation right before a teen graduates from high school. Parents know that, once their kid heads off to college, chances are some of them will prefer to vacation with their friends. Once their child has lived independently, everyone's role within the family will naturally shift.

This also should be a celebratory trip of accomplishment. It is an acknowledgement of everything your child has achieved during their 12 years in school. It also symbolizes the love, sacrifice and pride of parents. It's really not the end but should be a celebration of a family's future.

This particular family vacation is often looked to with much anticipation. At this point in life, many families are looking to plan their "dream" trips like an Alaskan cruise or tour of Europe. That said, it comes at a time when family finances may be stretched to the max. Once again, with a little bit of planning, this special vacation can exceed everyone's expectations.

As always, parents need to make their plans far in advance. With a small down payment there are often free vacation layaway plans to make payments more affordable.

Parents can also use group travel discounts to their advantage. (More on this topic in later chapters). Instead of planning expensive graduation parties, parents can invite family and friends to celebrate with them while on a great vacation together. Invite enough people and your entire family can get a free vacation, a free graduation party and your travel agent does all the work for you – nice deal!

Growing Families

I certainly do not want to conclude this section of the book discussing the "final" family vacation. In reality, family vacations don't really end when your kids go off to college. I can't tell you how many times a day we get requests for vacations with parents traveling with their adult children. Besides, without sounding melodramatic, it's the whole "circle of life" scenario. Couples become a family; children grow up, move out, find mates and turn parents into grandparents and the cycle returns to the beginning. Families simply continue to grow, evolve and include more people to love.

The travel needs of your family continue to grow and evolve too. Recognizing each of these different life stages will certainly help you to make wise and informed travel purchases.

The six family life stages are mainly focused on the children. In order for a family vacation to be fun, balanced and memorable, obviously the needs of parents must be considered. If a family vacation is planned properly it addresses the needs of all family members.

Parents work tremendously hard both on the job and at home to provide for their family. If a family vacation is "all about the kids" parents may return feeling gypped and little resentful. Vacation is a time all of us need to revive and feel alive. Every parent deserves a little "me" time. Every couple deserves a little "alone" time. Of course, when you travel with kids you are never "on vacation" from being a parent. Still, there are plenty of creative ways to plan and structure a vacation that has a little "me" time for both Mom and Dad, as well as a bit of romance for the couple together. Parents need not feel guilty about this if their children are safe, cared for and engaged having fun with peers. When parents give this gift of time to themselves, in turn it helps them achieve more balance in life and become better parents.

Vacations need to match the right ages and stages of your family in order for them to be fun and memorable events for all. If you purchased the wrong fitting vacation, it's not like a pair of jeans. You cannot bring it back to the store with your receipt for a full refund. And remember, vacations cost a whole lot more than a pair of jeans!

Use these six family life stages as a bit of a guideline to help you set priorities for your own family. They will also help you plan new and unique adventures as your family grows. Again, most families have members at different life stages at any given time, so compromises may need to be made in order to come to a fair and balanced decision.

« Chapter Six »

REAL WORLD FAMILY VACATION PLANNING

Definition: *Family – a group consisting of parents and children living together in a household.*

This definition of a "family" leaves much to interpretation. I hesitate to use the word "special" for the families discussed in this section. Truth be told many of these families are more "normal" than a typical two-parent mom/dad household.

Staying true to our six theme, there are also six groups of different types of families. If you find that your family "fits" into one of these categories, you will need to consider a few more things when planning your next vacation.

Life happens no matter how we plan. The only thing we're all certain about is that life is full of surprises.

Life forces families to evolve. It can certainly change our own personal definition of the people we call "family." I never planned to be a single mom with three kids. I also never planned on getting re-married. My best friend never expected that her child would be transgender. Another dear friend expected she'd

117

find a good husband and start a family. Instead she became a mom by in vitro fertilization. My cousin never imagined he'd be raising his two girls on his own, a widower at age 35.

I apologize in advance if I upset any reader's religious, political or moral points of view here. It is not my intention to shock, upset or cause any sort of controversy. As mentioned, it has been my own experience over the years that life often presents us with surprises that we might find hard to even imagine. Even if these unique family travel situations do not affect your family today, it's possible your family situation may change in the future. If these issues do not affect your immediate family, no doubt you know someone who could be helped by this information. My goal here is to promote understanding and help ALL parents get out and experience the world with their kids.

For years, the travel industry had its own definition of "family," which was typically "two adults and two kids under the age of 12." Many vacation brochures will picture a "typical" family of four at the beach – mom, dad, son and daughter enjoying a carefree day. They all have airbrushed perfect tans, white swimwear, and are walking along a perfect, deserted beach. Who ARE these people? I'm sure they are out there because I haven't heard of any false advertising claims. Still they don't look like any family I personally know!

I often joke that the families I normally work with have much more in common with the hit TV show "Modern Family" than the families seen in travel ad photos. If you picture that beloved cast, you'll appreciate some of the challenges we travel agents address in making some of our special families happy.

Thankfully, in recent years, the travel industry has finally caught on to the idea that the definition of a family is not typical and has changed dramatically in recent times. Accepting the fact that most traveling families are not "typical" has meant hoteliers, theme parks and cruise lines are beginning to evolve travel products, experiences and pricing that cater to a much broader range of families. (Thank goodness!)

BIG FAMILIES

"Two's company, three's a crowd"... This saying is very true when it is applied to family vacations. If parents have one or two children, it's all good. Your family fits the travel industry definition of the word "family" along with most hotel rooms and cruise ship cabins. Once you bring your third bundle of joy into this world and become a family of five, your family vacation choices have become limited and your travel budget has increased. So many parents are shocked when they go to book their first vacation with three kids. With each additional child you add to your family, the more challenging vacation planning will become.

It sounds silly, right? Take a look around at school drop-off, the mall or the next time you take the family out for a Happy Meal. Notice how many families there are out with three or more kids. For many years, the travel industry has been oblivious to this fact. Their standard, working definition of a "family" = two adults and two kids under the age of 12. This meant most family hotel rooms consisted of two double beds (or queen beds), one for the parents and the other for the kids to share.

Many hotels will not allow extra people to share the same hotel room, no matter how small those people may be. Often this is due to established local occupancy and fire codes. So what does this mean for parents who want to vacation with three, four or more kids?

It means, your family of five (or more) will require TWO hotel rooms.

But wait, it gets a bit worse...

Most hotels set their room fees based on "double adult rate" instead of charging a flat amount. If you think like a hotelier it will make a little bit more sense. They calculate all of their costs... housekeeping, laundry, maintenance, electric, water, profit, etc. For a hotelier it costs practically the same for one person to use the room as it does for two people to share the space. This is why you'll see rates like "single supplement," which is as much, or almost the same, as if two adults were sleeping in that room.

If you're a family with two adults and, say, three kids ages three, six and eight according to the rules your family will require two rooms, and it also means one family member will be paying a single adult rate and one of your kids will be paying a double adult rate.

Then it gets even more worse...

Of course, a family needing two rooms will want two rooms right next to each other and, ideally, connected by a door for both security reasons and togetherness. As far as a hotel is concerned, this is something guests can "request" but it is never a guarantee. Adjoining rooms may not be available at the time your family arrives to check in. Many hotels are built without doors between rooms. Parents are often surprised to realize that some of the largest resorts only have a handful of rooms with an adjoining door. If your family is traveling on a school holiday odds are, your chances of getting the room(s) you want are probably slim to none. No doubt you will probably find your family down the hall from one another, or even on another floor. With a cruise ship, you can at least confirm your specific cabins at the time of your reservation. This means if you book adjoining cabins then you are guaranteed two cabins next to one another with a door.

When larger families understand the costs of needing that extra room along with facing the idea of separation, many choose to invite grandparents or another family along to join them. This turns your vacation into what we travel agents would call a blended or multi-generational trip. If your child ends up sharing a room with an uncle, aunt and cousin, we can easily divide up costs so that everyone pays their fair share, even when your relatives may be flying in from a different part of the country.

As a mother of three, I feel your pain and I'm on your side. The good news is that the travel industry is slowly beginning to catch on to the idea that today's families need more space and want to be together. More and more resorts are offering rooms for families of five and even six. Of course, these rooms are in high demand so parents need to book early to avoid disappointment.

Other hotels are "wising up" to how the cruise ships do things and are now offering an upgraded room category called "guaranteed adjoining" and, as the name implies, these are two rooms connected to each other with a door in between. Every hotel offering this type of room may call it by a different name, like "family suite" perhaps, which adds to the confusion. It's important to either know the resort or have a detailed room description to ensure you are getting two rooms with an adjoining door. Usually this is one room with a king-size bed for Mom and Dad, which connects with a door to a second room that has two double beds for the kids.

Many newer resorts and even cruise ships are being built with more flexible floor plans. For example, "railroad rooms," each with connecting doors and larger floor plans. With doors locked, each individual room, studios and suite can be sold separately. Sold as a block of rooms together with all the doors unlocked, these suites can accommodate up to 12 family members. Of course, these types of rooms are considered upgrades and they do come with a higher price tag and are always in high demand.

Wait! There is still one more thing to remember...

Some hotels do define "children" as age 17 and under, and there are some that will accommodate larger families. Even Disney's latest Art of Animation resort in Disney World will accommodate a family of six with teens.

With larger resorts and all-inclusive properties, the ones that do allow families of five or six to share the same room with their parents stipulate that all children must be under the age of 12. Once your oldest offspring turns 13, it becomes even more challenging finding hotel rooms that fit. This is when a family cruise may sound more appealing. Many family cruise lines do offer cabins that are family of five- and six-friendly. The difference is that most cruise ships charge by the number of guests sharing the same cabin, not by age. The first and second passengers pay a higher fare and the third, fourth, fifth or sixth passengers pay lower rates. Families traveling with three or four teens can save substantially with a cruise vacation compared to a land-based resort stay.

SINGLE PARENT VACATIONS

Whether by choice or by circumstance, being a single parent is never easy. Single parents often find themselves playing the role of both mom and dad regardless of their gender. Speaking from firsthand experience, I know how easy it is to feel quickly outnumbered and overwhelmed. Double the work means double the need for a vacation.

There are many ways to end up in the role of being a single parent. It could be a birth decision, foster care or an elected adoption. Single parenthood may be a result of separation, divorce or death.

Even married couples can find themselves "single" when it comes to travel regulations. Perhaps Mom will be attending an international business conference in London. Her company will be paying for her travel. It make financial sense to take advantage of the situation and have dad and the kids fly over to join her for a few days of vacation time once she's done with work. In this situation, this married, biological dad would be treated as a single parent traveling alone with children and would need to present additional paperwork proving his status at immigration.

Most of what is discussed here has to do with overseas travel and proof of citizenship. Again, every family's circumstances are different and they need to understand how their situation affects their travel plans. A road trip to a neighboring state for a water park weekend has the potential for serious consequences if your custody agreement does not allow for this, or if the trip wasn't cleared in advance with foster care.

Regardless of your circumstances, there some extra plans and a bit more proof that must be taken into account when you make your travel plans. It may perhaps feel like an unfair twist of fate that single parents need to do twice as much work to prove they alone care for the kids. Remember these extra steps have been put into place to safeguard kids and prevent illegal abductions.

All passengers, regardless of their age, will require a passport to travel outside of the United States. Parents of children under the age of 16 must apply for passports on behalf of their children. Basically all parents will need written proof of two important facts as part of the passport application. First parents must to prove their child is a US citizen. Secondly they must prove their own parental relationship to that child. Again, depending on your unique family circumstances, single parents will need additional paperwork and legal proof of their parental relationship. Http:// www. travel.state.gov is where parents can find forms, fees, photo requirements and necessary requirements for single parents.

In addition to your child's passport application, single parents will often need to present additional documentation at airport check-ins, cruise embarkations and border crossings. The way to prove your parental rights depends on the reason why you are a single parent.

Depending on your circumstances, in addition to a valid US passport, single or lone parents traveling abroad with children under the age of 16 may be required to present:

- Death certificate of biological parent

- Full custody agreement

- Notarized letter from co-parent authorizing permission to travel

- Final adoption papers

Each and every country has its own rules regarding acceptable forms of proof. Be sure to inform yourself of the rules in advance. Some countries may require legal papers to be translated into the local language. Even if the rules of entry for the country do not specify the need for additional documentation for single parents, as both a single mom and travel agent, I tend to operate on the idea of "better safe than sorry." It's far better to carry extra documentation with you than to be called into question at the airport or immigration.

The information presented here comes from years of working as a family travel planner. I am not a lawyer and do not pretend to give legal advice. Every family's circumstances are different as are the laws where they live. Use this information as a guideline and seek appropriate legal advice when necessary.

Often excited parents head off full steam ahead making reservations. They invest vacation dollars only to find themselves disappointed and often financially penalized when they realize they do not have the proper travel documentation. Remember, it is the responsibility of all travelers to have the right travel documents. If you arrive at the airport or cruise terminal without it you will not be allowed to board your plane or ship. It also means you will forfeit the entire cost of your vacation. Lack of proper documentation is not covered by travel insurance. You will find yourself out of pocket for the entire cost of your trip.

Single parents may find themselves in legal limbo. They want to plan ahead for a vacation and save as much money as possible. Custody cases may still be under review. There is no guarantee will have their legal cases settled and paperwork in order by the time they depart for their vacation. In situations like this, single parents can go ahead confidently with their reservations as long as they have purchased "cancel for any reason" insurance. This type of coverage usually costs a little bit more than traditional travel protection coverage, and must be purchased at the same time you confirm your reservations. As the name implies, you can simply cancel your travel plans, right up until the time of your departure for a full refund of your vacation costs. This covers your vacation investment just in case all of the legalities are not worked out prior to your departure.

Speaking of costs, single parents often have a hard time understanding the travel term "double adult rate." Most hotels and cruise ships do not charge a flat fee per night. Instead hotels and cruise lines determine the nightly cost of their rooms depending on how many people share that one room. Hoteliers have calculated their costs like electricity, water usage, maintenance, laundry, insurance and housekeeping down to the penny. From a travel industry point of view, it pretty much costs the same to clean and maintain a room for one person as it does for two people. That is why, even if you are one adult sleeping in a room, you pay as much or almost as much as if two people were sleeping in that same room. Also, according to these "double adult rate" rules, every room must have at least two adults (or adult rates charged) before any kids rates are allowed.

So how does this hotel rule affect single-parent families when they go on vacation? Let's say you are a single mom traveling with two kids, ages six and eight. According to the double adult rate, even though both children are under the age of 12, technically one of the kids has to pay a full adult rate according to the hotel rules. Remember, this isn't the hotel trying to discriminate against single parents, it's about calculating business costs and profits for the hotel.

Of course one way parents get around this rule is to invite an adult friend or family member along with you on vacation and ask them to pay their share. Not only will this help your budget but it may help your sanity as far as having an extra pair of hands with the kids. Having another adult along for the fun will also help Mom or Dad enjoy some adult conversation and not feel like a third wheel. Remember every family vacation needs balance.

Many single-parent families may want to vacation with another single-parent family in similar circumstances. This too is a great idea but success often depends on the number of adults and kids traveling together. Often the main motivation for traveling together is to save on budget, only to find that together these families will have too many people to fit occupancy rules for one room. Having to upgrade to a suite in order to fit everyone may be fun but may not result in any savings in the long run.

There are some hotels that do offer single-parent rates. This means that adults pay adult prices no matter how many are staying in a room and kids under a certain age will pay kids' prices. Disney resorts have this policy. Adults pay adult rates and kids under 17 pay children's rates. Of course, when it comes to park admission, anyone over the age of nine is considered an adult. There are also a handful of hotels and all-inclusive resorts that will offer single-parent deals too. These special rates are usually during low seasons like September and May, so it may be tricky when you're dealing with a school calendar. Those that do offer these deals throughout the year will only offer a handful of rooms at this special rate so it is necessary to plan far in advance.

DIVORCED FAMILIES

Divorced family vacations are a bit different even though many of the travel rules are the same as single-parent trips. To use a trendy term, a divorced family vacation means there was a "conscious uncoupling" of that family. No doubt there are a few extremely cooperative and well-balanced teams of two unattached parents who will vacation together with their biological children, but this is certainly not the norm. With divorced parents it usually means one parent will be vacationing with the kids and the other parent will not.

Divorce and separation are delicate and stressful times for any family. Hopefully it is a time when grown-ups can indeed act in an adult way and put the needs and the well-being of their children first—ahead of their own feelings. Parents are not required to live together or even like each other but they do need to figure out a healthy way to be able to co-parent their children until they reach adulthood.

Even in the very best of circumstances there is so much to plan and think about when going through all the legalities of a divorce. Vacation planning is not something parents normally consider during this process but it can become a major issue shortly after.

The topic of vacation rights should come into play as couples discuss the custody and visiting terms of their divorce agreement. If possible, discuss it in advance and get rules for vacations in writing ahead of time. Where and when are co-parents allowed to travel with the kids? Is it okay for the kids to travel overseas and are the parents willing to cooperate in the application for passports? If the parents have new significant others, are they allowed to travel with the kids? If you only get to see your children during certain school holidays, this may in turn increase the overall cost of your vacation. If you and your ex-spouse are living a great distance from each other, issues like kids flying alone to meet a parent for vacation add to concerns. Will the children be able to visit or vacation with grandparents or other members of your ex-spouse's family? Should emergency medical care be necessary for your children while away on vacation, who has the right to make any lifesaving decisions?

If vacations were never a topic of discussion at the conference table, then be sure to discuss it with either your lawyer or co-parent before confirming travel reservations for your children. This will certainly save you any last-minute disappointment or cancellation penalties. Again, as suggested in the previous chapter on single parents, make sure you have purchased "cancel for any reason" travel protection, especially if you think your ex may try to pull a power play at the very last minute.

Even if your divorce is a friendly one, families who have shared or joint custody will often require a letter of permission from a co-parent in order to travel with their children. These letters do not need to be lengthy or very formal but they do need to be notarized. Depending on your vacation destination, some foreign countries do require these letters of permission to be translated into their native language.

Here is an example of a permission letter:

To whom it may concern –

I (your name) give permission for my children (their name[s]) to travel with their (father/mother) to (destination) for their vacation from (departure date) until (return date).

Signature_____
Date_____

Notary
Signature_____

____

Again, this advice is coming from a travel agent and a divorced mom. This sample of a permission letter I share here is one that I have used in the past with my own children to travel overseas. That said, I am not a lawyer. I highly recommend that you always consult with your family's legal counsel who fully understands the legal needs and rights of your specific family situation. You may also want to include permission to make important medical decisions for your children while on vacation.

Besides the legal implications that divorced families face when traveling, parents must also consider the emotional needs of their children. Divorce can be a tumultuous time of change for kids in so many ways. For some it can mean moving, a change of school, friends, pets and always a change in the life they knew before. Change means uncertainty and anxiety for kids. Some kids are not old enough to voice their concerns, while others may not yet be able to verbally communicate their fears.

Even though vacations are ideally meant to mean a carefree week or two of fun, to children coping with a divorce they may meant yet another change or even more stress. Even though parents may desperately need a vacation to escape, be alert and sensitive as to whether or not a vacation may be ideal for the way your child is feeling right then. Be sure to check with your children's teachers or counselors. Ask for their advice and suggestions for making this transition easier for your kids.

Getting your kid(s) involved from the very beginning of any vacation planning will help them to feel empowered. Plan some quiet, undistracted time to talk with your children about their idea of taking a vacation. Be sensitive to their concerns. Hopefully both co-parents can present the idea of vacation to the kids at the same time. If kids see that parents are setting the example, working together and showing that both are okay with the idea, it is usually less stressful for kids. Then again, you may not want to speak with your ex but your child may need to know that they can speak to them every day they are away. Again, the more you can plan and coordinate communication in advance like times to call, Skype or Google Hangouts, and WiFi usage, the easier it will hopefully be for everyone.

Even if your ex refuses to play by the rules, allow your children to express their needs. For example, if your ex doesn't want to take the time for daily calls from the kids, perhaps help your children create a photo album they can show their parent the next time they are together.

Divorce is often a time when kids may act up and certainly test the limits. If both co-parents can have a joint conversation and present a united outline of acceptable behaviors for the kids in advance—wonderful. At the very least, kids deserve to know and understand the rules prior to leaving home along with the consequences for their behavior. As long as everyone plays fair it should all work out fine. If not, then it's time to get lawyers and counselors involved to mediate and correct the situation.

Parents also need to know their own limits. I speak from experience when I say that it can feel completely overwhelming to think about traveling with young children and to keep them safe, especially when it's one parent with multiple kids. Do not be afraid to ask for help. As a parent, you need to find the confidence to be the group travel leader for your family. This can mean planning a vacation with some sort of child care or activity program. It can mean asking a trusted friend or family member to travel with you. It may mean leaving an unruly child with your ex, a trusted friend or family member until that kid earns the right to a vacation by a show of good behavior. It's about finding the right solution that works best for the well-being of your entire family.

Keep the faith, divorced parents. It generally does get easier. The first vacation after parents get divorced, or decide to separate, can be challenging. Mostly it's because this vacation is a trip into unknown territory. I'm not talking about the destination for your trip. I'm talking about family dynamics. Hopefully, with some compassionate cooperation, the journey will be a good one.

BLENDED FAMILIES

Definition: *A blended family is one that includes a couple and their children from this and all of their previous relationships.*

This term has been updated since the days of the Brady Bunch. Back in the day, the term "step" to describe a family member without a direct blood tie was used, often with adjectives like "wicked" or "ugly."

In today's world, the term "blended family" can also be used to describe families in which some of the children are biological offspring and others are not. Adoptive members of the family may or may not be blood-related.

Having one big happy family is certainly a blessing, but it does come with some unique challenges when it comes to vacation planning. Once again, some of these are rules and regulations that need to be followed, while other considerations focus on everyone's enjoyment.

As mentioned in previous chapters concerning single parents and divorced parents, many of the same rules come into play with blended families. Let's say two divorced people with kids decided to marry and plan a destination wedding. Besides planning the date and location of this event, both the bride and groom must consider the custody and visitation rules set forth in their prior divorce agreement. Again, depending on their individual circumstances, along with the attitudes and cooperation of their previous partners, this could mean a simple letter of permission from co-parents or full-on legal custody battles.

Another example may be a married couple with a biological child of their own who choose to adopt the mother's niece and nephew to keep them out of the foster care system. Additional legal documents will be required to obtain passports or travel as a blended family.

In our case, a blended family included my brave husband who married me when my kids were age 11, 13 and 15. Never having had children of his own from a prior marriage, he suddenly found himself the instant father of teenagers. The first time we all traveled together, it was certainly an "adjustment" for everyone.

Once the legal issues of a blended family have been prepped and addressed, it's time to enjoy a fun vacation together. The adults are probably of one heart and mind. No doubt their love was the reason for creating this new blended family. A marriage between two people, though, does not guarantee that everyone in the family shares the same feeling of togetherness and is all "Kumbaya."

The first important reality check here is the realization that a family vacation will not cure any existing family problems. Real life is often far different from scenarios portrayed on TV sitcoms. Being in paradise or the "happiest place on earth" doesn't guarantee that everyone will miraculously cooperate and treat each other nicely. If your blended family is having issues respecting one another, this problem needs to be addressed with professional counseling before ever leaving home. Denying the obvious will generally result in a trip full of anxiety, stress and even more resentment. Work on solving your family problems first and then celebrate your newfound togetherness and solutions with a family vacation.

Togetherness is a result of respecting everyone's individuality. Do not tolerate or promote any teasing or bullying. Jokes may be made in jest, but if taken to heart by a child, they can cause lasting personal pain. Parents need to be very mindful to avoid any temptation to bad-mouth ex-spouses or make comparisons to previous families/relationships or past vacation experiences. Also, for the sake of the children, be respectful of traditions from previous families. Parents will need to decide if these traditions will be carried over into the new blended family, or if this new family should create some new traditions. Getting the kids involved in these types of family interactions is another simple way of helping them to become active participants in their new family. Kids who know and understand the rules have a much better chance of playing by them. If everyone in the family is free to speak their mind and share concerns in a safe atmosphere, it will do a great deal in helping the family come together.

As mentioned previously, make sure kids can stay in touch with co-parents and family members back home. Open and respectful communication is the key to making kids feel comfortable in new situations.

Parents of blended families want everyone to "just get along." Of course everything costs more for larger families. There is the temptation to cut corners and costs whenever possible. A bigger, blended family often needs bigger accommodations. They also need a bit more "personal space" than a smaller or traditional family. Having neutral corners to take "time out" from others can mean a world of difference when it comes to easing tensions. Blended parents may need to book larger accommodations with multiple bedrooms to help keep the peace. It may mean a quality vacation for four nights instead of seven nights with continuous arguments.

One sure way blended family vacations work is when every single member of the family is celebrated and made to feel important. Again, these individual solutions will be as different and as individual as every blended family out there. The level of participation will also depend on every child's age and level of understanding. Some are simple ideas, like a small surprise present for everyone one morning. Another idea would be to let each family member choose a fun activity every day of the trip. Letting others know your favorite activities can help to open lines of communication and get everyone involved. Perhaps each night for dinner, one family member can be crowned VIP for that night and enjoy their favorite cake while everyone takes turns making a toast as to why that person is extra special. These VIP gestures can seem small in the scheme of the universe but can make a world of difference to every member of the family.

GLBT FAMILY VACATIONS

Call it a "gaby boom," but more and more gay, lesbian, bisexual and transgender (GLBT) couples are looking to vacation with their rainbow families. GLBT family households are numbered at about three million. From a travel industry perspective, the US Department of Commerce estimates this sector of the population to spend an average of $70 billion annually on travel, and a very large percentage of this group have passports in hand. With more and more states recognizing gay marriage, the number of GLBT families is expected to grow in the foreseeable future.

The GLBT community has always had their favorite vacation destination spots, specialized tours and cruise events. Destinations like San Francisco, Miami, Vegas, Provincetown and others have embraced the GLBT community. These cities draw vacationing members of the GLBT community from all over the globe, especially those who live in rural areas where they face discrimination for being different.

In many ways, GLBT travel is very similar to straight travel. Generally, GLBT singles want to party and have fun. Once they find their partners, it's about togetherness, romance and building a life together. As soon as GLBTs partners become parents, it's all about their kids.

Every family, regardless of sexual preferences, has the same universal dreams for their children. They want their kids to feel loved, safe and happy. All parents want to create fond vacation memories with their kids. The last thing GLBT families want to deal with is vacation discrimination.

Bear in mind here, the term "GLBT families" doesn't necessarily mean GLBT parents with kids. It can also mean straight families with GLBT children. Some transgender kids recognize their gender identity from the time there are toddlers. Some teens may already have come out to their parents early on about their sexual preferences. Even if GLBT travel issues don't necessarily affect your immediate family, odds are, it may influence your extended family vacation. At the very least, you're probably very likely to meet GLBT families at the resort pool or beach.

The tricky bit for these families is that the typical GLBT tours, travel companies, cruises and vacation packages to gay friendly destinations are not "kid friendly." The same holds true in reverse. "Family friendly" resorts and destinations in the past have not always rolled out the welcome mat for GLBT families.

In addition, many global destinations have strict anti-gay laws like certain Caribbean destinations, Russia and Egypt. For example, New York City has laws on the books allowing transgenders to use the public bathroom of their choice, but the state of New York does not.

Thankfully the travel industry is slowly beginning to recognize that the term "family vacation" does not mean "one size fits all." Global brands like Hilton and Marriott are creating vacation products and packages specifically designed for GLBT families. Disney parks have been hosting "gay days" since 1991. These are usually held in June to coincide with gay-pride month. In July 2014, Disney partnered with the Orlando tourism board for the first "Family Outfest" Orlando, along with Nickelodeon Suites Resort, Macy's and Hilton Orlando Lake Buena Vista. This event was specifically geared for kid-friendly fun for GBLT families.

Same as with straight families, safety and comfort are paramount with GLBT parents when they vacation with their children. The perfect destination or accommodation needs to be both family-friendly and welcoming to members of the GLBT community. No doubt GLBT parents have already had age-appropriate discussions with their kids about tolerance, discrimination and acceptance. Even though a GLBT family-friendly vacation spot has been chosen, chances are your family will be interacting with people from many different countries and cultures when visiting tourist destinations. This means kids may not be completely insulated from interactions with discriminatory individuals. This makes vacation time a good time to review these topics of discussion with your kids. It will certainly help them be able to react and handle things properly should they happen to encounter this type of situation.

Legally, GLBT families have similar obligations as any other family, especially when traveling overseas with kids. Does your holiday destination recognize your marriage or union without formal adoption papers? Parents will need to prove their identity and parental relationship, especially with different last names. Birth certificates along with foster or adoption papers, marriage licenses or domestic partnership agreements will necessary at immigration along with passports.

Transgender people have a few additional considerations. The transitioning process may take several years. During this time, many transgender individuals may appear in public despite the legal name and gender listed on their birth certificate, driver's license or passport. Once fully transitioned, they can petition the court to legally change their name and gender. Until this happens, it can cause some confusion with travel, especially airport security.

As mentioned in earlier chapters, when it comes to airport security, the legal names, date of birth and gender of all passengers MUST match exactly with their ID and plane tickets. For this reason, the TSA suggests that all transgender passengers appear at the airport dressed according to the gender on their travel documents. If a transgender passenger chooses to appear differently, this can cause confusion and is reason for additional screening. Prosthetics used by transgender individuals can set off airport imaging scanners that can require extra luggage checks and pat downs. Any passenger can ask for privacy when it comes to a baggage check or pat down. At no time will a passenger be requested to show or remove any prosthetics. If a pat down is required, it will be performed by a TSA officer of the same gender as listed on the passenger's passport or official ID.

From a travel agent's perspective, it is our responsibility to make sure all the vacations we arrange for our clients go off without hitch. Most GLBT families which I have worked with have been very open and honest. In turn, this certainly helps me to ultimately help make them happy.

Of course there are also those family situations where we agents are forced to ask "delicate" questions about relationships, as well as preferred sleeping arrangements. It's not that we're trying to get all up in your family's business. Agents who have specialized in family travel long enough know better than to ever "assume" anything. Ultimately, our goal is to ensure that all security obligations are met and that our families have a fun, hassle-free adventure—together. The more we know about the likes, dislikes and personalities of all of our families, the better we can partner with them to ensure that their vacation dreams exceed their expectations.

MULTI-GENERATIONAL VACATIONS AND FAMILY REUNIONS

A multi-generational vacation is one of the new trendy terms being used in the travel business today. It's a bit different from a family reunion. By strict definition, a multi-generational vacation is one vacation with three or more generations of people traveling on the same itinerary... think grandparents, parents and kids.

The term has changed because travel patterns have changed. In years past, families grew up in the same area. Parents and kids lived near grandparents and siblings. In some neighborhoods, extended families shared the same multi-dwelling house.

In today's world, immediate families find themselves spread out across the country. Grandma and grandpa have retired to the Carolinas. Their son, his wife and their three kids live in Chicago. Their daughter and her eight-year-old girl live in NYC. Everyone wants to see one another so they all gather for a vacation. Vacationing together means the kids are entertained and everyone has their own room and privacy. No one person is stuck with all the cooking and cleaning. It makes perfect sense!

The trick to planning a successful multi-generational trip is balance and compromise. The needs, wishes and abilities of every traveler must be taken into consideration in the planning stages. Everyone may want to do a white water rafting trip but Grandma has a bad hip. Compromises will need to be made so that the trip can be inclusive for everyone. Perhaps a family cruise with a river-raft excursion in one of the Caribbean ports may be a better compromise. Everyone gets to vacation with Grandma and she can hit the spa on port day as everyone goes rafting.

Some families have phenomenal decision-making capabilities and amazing teamwork. I admire these families. Other families are incredibly dysfunctional when it comes to agreeing on something. I do speak of this from personal experience. Getting everyone to agree, or even compromise, can be a monumental task. Once again, setting some fair play rules in advance can certainly help this situation. In keeping with our theme of six, here are six tips for getting everyone in your group on the same page...

1. **Appoint a group leader** – Whether this person is the one paying the bill, the person whose birthday everyone is celebrating or the family member born with the most organizational genes, that is entirely up to your group. Regardless of who gets elected, it is important for many reasons to have a leader.

   Your leader can help to keep everyone on task as far responsibilities and due dates are concerned, and act as a point of contact. From a travel perspective, the group leader's name is often used to link reservations. This helps keep rooms close together or ensure everyone's dinner reservations. Having one person with the final decision-making authority to break tie votes will also help to keep the peace and avoid anarchy.

2. **Use modern technology to get old-fashioned answers** – Schedule family meetings using tools like Skype or Google Hangout so that everyone can have face-to-face meetings even if you are miles apart. Set up a private Facebook group for your vacation and be sure to invite and include your travel agent. We often will set up a private Facebook group and send invites as a courtesy to our clients. Depending on the situation, we have built personal websites to help you promote your trip for family and friends.

   Having your travel agent involved right from the start can help keep your group on task as well as on their best behavior. This keeps the lines of communication open not only with vacation planning but also with facilitating answers for last-minute departure questions, which always pop up. It is a tremendous help allowing your travel agent to work efficiently in order to answer all questions quickly. It's also fun during and after the trip, allowing everyone to swap and share photos and videos. There is no greater reward for a dedicated travel agent than to see proof of their happy families enjoying vacation time together!

3. **Begin with the Six Basic Guideline Questions** – This means each traveling family should fill out one of the travel forms found in the first chapter of this book. Use these important questions as a discussion format to keep everyone on task during Skype meetings or Google Hangouts. In this way, each family is responsible right from the start for ensuring everyone's name is spelled right, passport expiration dates are correct, etc. It will help to keep all your family's information organized and it will certainly make your travel agent's life infinitely easier.

4. **Have an HONEST Discussion about Budget** – Of course, budget is part of the initial six guideline questions for each family, but it must be discussed in the context of the group.

In some cases, a generous family member may pay for everyone. In other cases, the budgets of each individual household may come into play. Perhaps each family will be paying for their own travel but Grandma wishes to treat all the grandkids to a swim with the dolphins. This is the time to decide who will be paying for what.

Sometimes group members may need to contribute to the cause in order to ensure that every member of the family is included. As long as the travel companies get paid at the end of the day, your travel agent can divide the payments in any way and conquer the day. Just know, if you plan to pay for another family member who is listed under a separate reservation number, you may be required to sign a third-party authorization form. This is a standard procedure by many travel companies intended as a security measure and a way to prevent unlawful credit card use and fraud.

Depending on how many people are traveling, your group may be entitled to discounts or perks. Discounts can be applied to everyone or they can be used for the benefit of a particular family member. Once again, if your group starts out with an honest conversation about budgets and payments, it makes it much easier to allocate any earned discounts.

5. **Set Deadlines for Decisions** – Everyone is distracted and living busy lives so do set a deadline for when travel decisions must be made. If too much time elapses, then the quotes your travel agent gave you will no longer be valid and your group will need to start the process all over again.

6. **Be a Team Player** – Decisions never happen in the face of confusion. Distractions slow the wheels of progress. If everyone is surfing independently online for new "ideas" and different vacation package deals that are all over the map, it will only delay progress, cause frustration and usually increase the price everyone pays.

   Being a responsible team player also means meeting any payment deadlines, being on time for events, and keeping a positive attitude. When you travel as part of a group, it's not all about you.

The term "multi-generational vacation" speaks about age. It really doesn't speak about size or the number of family members traveling together. A multi-gen trip might mean a single room shared by a grandparent, parent and child. It can also mean a huge family reunion with hundreds of members.

Group Discounts

Group travel could be a complete topic for another book. Discounts offered to large numbers of people traveling together can be used to benefit families in so many creative ways. I will do my best to simplify some of the rules and share the basics. Once you understand some of these rules, I trust group discounts will spur your imagination and you'll begin to see some of their real benefits, especially when it comes to obtaining your family's travel dreams.

Again, the travel industry never makes it easy. Each and every hotel, theme park, and cruise ship has their own rules, and there are different rules for different types of groups. The fine print contracts for terms and conditions, as well as travel insurance coverage also differs when dealing with groups compared with individual vacations.

When it comes to hotel rooms and cruise ship cabins, discounted rates are once again based on double adult occupancy. Children's rates or say third and fourth person cruise cabin rates rarely count towards any group discounts.

Often a group discount means "free" spaces allotted to the group. This means certain individuals may travel free or that a credit can be applied to everyone. The word *"free"* is in quotes because honestly, very few things in this world are completely free. Taxes will still need to be paid on any "free" space earned by the group.

Let's face it, the government never gives anybody a free ride when it comes to paying taxes. Airport departure taxes, cruise taxes and port fees can indeed cost a few hundred dollars depending on the specifics of your trip. As you are planning your budget, remember you may still have to pay for your taxes or other components of your trip unless you have enough people in your group to qualify for additional discounts.

In addition to the "freebies" gained by the numbers of travelers you have, everyone in your group may pay a cheaper fare or receive additional perks for being part of a group. Hotels and resorts will often offer a lower rate for "buying in bulk" as part of a group. Cruise ships may offer extra amenities like a free group cocktail party to celebrate a special event.

People are often surprised to learn that group airfares are rarely cheaper than what everyone could find online booking their flights online. Airlines will block seats together and will maintain a certain standard price for a specific amount of time so that prices do not constantly fluctuate. Making sure that everyone pays the same price for their flights helps keep everything fair when dealing with a large group traveling together. Remember, even though flight prices may not be cheaper, there is the potential for earning free space if your group reaches a certain number of passengers.

So how can you use these group travel benefits to help your family?

1. **Free Space Can Be Used Different Ways** – The dollar amount can be split to lower everyone's cost even more. The entire amount can be used towards the fare of one family member. Grandpa gets a free cruise for his birthday, or the family with four kids can use this amount to help make their travel more affordable. The amount of free space that your group earns can even be used as a fundraiser or donated to charity.

2. **Plan Groups at Least One Year in Advance** – You need extra time when prepping for a group vacation. Many group vacations are annual events planned far in advance. You want to ensure that people you plan on inviting haven't already committed to their own vacations.

3. **Group Travel Doesn't Mean 24/7 Togetherness** – Unless that is what you prefer. Smaller family groups can feel free to invite extended family members, friends, co-workers, social media contacts and even advertise to strangers. You can invite everyone to partake in the specialized group activities or if you choose, you never have to interact with them while you're away. People you invite can take advantage of lower group rates and any perks. Many folks just enjoy it when others take care of all the travel planning. You and your family benefit by collecting more freebies. The more freebies you earn, the

less your family pays for your own vacation. I've had many families vacation for free just by inviting others to come along.

4. **Deposits and Deadlines** – Hotels, cruise ships and airlines will not simply block group space as a favor so that you can try to sell it to your friends and family. You must put your money where your mouth is. Be prepared to place a deposit. Many group leaders simply pay in full for their family vacation right at the beginning. This money acts as a "deposit" to hold a certain number of rooms or cruise cabins while they invite others. Other group leaders will pay as little as $50 per person or $100 per room to hold a certain number of rooms for a set amount of time. As long as you give back any unsold space by the deadline in your contract, group leaders are under no financial obligation and will get their money back (or have it applied to their own vacation).

5. **Group Discounts Are Not Just for Families** – Even though our discussion of group travel is listed here under multi-generational trips and family reunions, remember you don't have to be a family to enjoy group discounts. Anyone can start the ball rolling and can elect themselves as a travel group leader. Invent your own group and invite your book club, hobby groups, business meetings, play groups, kids' sports team, schoolmates, church members, etc. The more people you sign on, the more travel discounts you and your family will enjoy.

6. **Partner with an Experienced Travel Agent** – Earning a "free" vacation for you or your family can quickly spiral out of hand and become a full-time endeavor. You will need to ensure that every person you've invited has a great time and gets all of their questioned addressed. If your guests are not frequent travelers, there will be a LOT of questions. You will also need to protect yourself from any financial liabilities. This is why it is *extremely* important to partner with a travel agent who is experienced in group travel.

Your travel agent partner can help you with creative ideas for special events to help entice even more people to join you for a specialized vacation. Creating a "one of a kind" event means that people you invite or advertise to won't be able to get the same experience by purchasing their vacation somewhere else online.

Your travel agent does all the work while you take all the glory. When we work with a large group, we will even set up a website, offer free webinars and will even speak at live events to help you recruit larger followings. Again, depending on the projected size of your group, your travel agent should help you with some of the marketing as well as advertising costs.

Are you beginning to see the possibilities that group discounts can offer your family? If done properly, group travel can not only help you and your family vacation for free, it can even be a great way to earn extra income or raise funds for your favorite charitable cause.

Group travel can help your family fund travel dreams that may seem impossible or unattainable.

THE EVOLUTION OF FAMILY VACATIONS

Vacation circumstances will change each year for every type of family out there. It's a fact of life but our children grow up! Births, deaths, separations and marriages will change the portrait of every family over the years while, in turn, influencing each of our vacation needs, wishes and decisions.

Last year, your family may have been part of a larger group traveling to attend your sister's destination wedding. This year your parents plan on joining you and the kids for a week at the beach. Vacations next year might include a five-day trip skiing all together in Utah. The following year might necessitate a weeklong road trip through New England for you and your eldest to check out a few of the colleges she has on her radar.

145

Fearless Family Vacations

No matter what your vacation "WHY" is each year, now you'll have the planning skills to focus your travel planning to make the most of your family's time together. No matter what your circumstances or family's situation, you'll know how to fearlessly plan and create affordable trips.

« Chapter Seven »

SIX TYPES OF FAMILY TRIPS

Basically there are six types of family vacations. Don't let the titles here fool you into thinking these are generic, cookie-cutter vacations. They are simply categories for organizational purposes and only limited by your imagination.

A huge majority of destinations can be experienced in many different ways. If your family's dream is to visit Italy, it may be best for you to rent a villa, sightsee independently using public transport, take an escorted tour, sail on a cruise or even hike the Cinque Terre. The type or style of vacation your family ultimately chooses will be determined by all of the travel planning parameters we've a discussed in earlier chapters. Bottom line, you have lots of options when it comes to the types of vacations available.

Remember that, if a family member's age or limitations prevent you from a certain type or style of trip this year, it may be an idea that your family can "grow into" for a future vacation.

Needless to say, entire books have been written about each of these types of trips to specific destinations all over the planet.

Fearless Family Vacations

My last Amazon search returned well over 100 guidebook choices for Disney World Orlando alone.

What I hope to do here is to present family vacation ideas to help you understand available travel product options. In addition, I'll offer some general guidelines, considerations and tips to help point you in the right direction. I've said it before, there is not one single "best" vacation. Hopefully, this information will ultimately help you to find and plan the very best vacation that is perfect for your family.

FAMILY VACATION PACKAGES

Definition – *Two or more travel components necessary to create a trip or vacation.*

It is really important to grasp this definition. Understanding what this means will not only affect your budget but it will enable you to determine whether a travel deal is a good one or one that is completely bogus.

According to the definition, two or more travel components are needed to create a vacation package... so what is considered a component?

Let's think about what components your family will need to take a vacation:

- Flights

- Transportation or car rental

- A place to stay – hotel, cruise cabin, villa

- Sightseeing tours

- Admission tickets

According to our definition, by combining two or more of these components, anyone can create a vacation package. So why is this important?

If you believe everything you hear or see on TV, you'll save a ton of money by going online to any major travel website and booking a "vacation package." Combine your flights and hotel and save a bundle. Of course, everything you hear on TV or read online is 100% true, right? Think again my friend...

The travel industry spends millions of dollars on marketing and sales promotions. Most want to protect the integrity of their brand and their pricing. Many hotels and cruise lines will enforce their advertised prices and not take kindly to anyone offering discounts or rebates. They believe discounts "de-value" how the public views their products.

For example, Disney has extremely strict advertising rules about how advertisers and travel agents present and advertise their prices. If someone tries to discount Disney, they will be banned from doing business with the parks faster than two shakes of a mouse's tail!

In an effort to sell airline seats, hotels, rental cars, etc., the travel industry needed a way to offer discounts without "devaluing" the normal retail price of their products and services. This is why they created "vacation packages." By advertising ONE price for two or more vacation components, any discounts that were offered would be "hidden" from the consumer. The vacation package was then marketed as a convenience and a discount for the customer.

Years back, consumers would find tons of great "vacation package deals" in the Sunday travel section of their newspapers. Major travel players would contract with one another and hide any discounts in these package deals.

The Internet arrived and consumer travel websites like Expedia, Travelocity and Orbitz had the technology to sell travel products faster online. The airlines, hotels and car rental companies signed contracts with these companies, and these websites "packaged" these travel components for online sales. Another version of this hidden discount pricing was Priceline with its "name your own price" program. The name of the hotel you'll be sleeping in is hidden until after you pay your lower price.

As time evolved, airlines and hotel companies built their own consumer direct websites. Often this was a much more direct and cheaper form of distribution for them. The goal was to capture customer loyalty. Travel brands wanted folks to come directly to their websites instead of a major travel website where they run the risk of losing a customer to one of their competitors. Now a travel company can offer a deal or discount faster and more efficiently with its social media fans.

Today there is less cooperation between travel brands. Basically Expedia and Priceline have gobbled up most of their competitor websites. This means most of the prices customers spend hours searching for online all come from the same two sources. Pricing is far more transparent. This means there are fewer great vacation package deals available for consumers.

Yes, there are still a few instances where buying a vacation flight + car rental or flight + hotel will save you a few bucks. The problem is that millions of marketing dollars have brainwashed consumers to believe that buying a vacation package is ALWAYS cheaper. Few consumers bother to check one-way flights or price vacation components separately. DIY travel planners will blindly book a vacation package online and will sleep soundly thinking they got a great deal when in fact they paid a lot more money than they should have paid.

The only way to know for sure that you've found the best price is to be an informed consumer. Make sure you are comparing "apples to apples." Get a total package price of your family's airfare, hotel stay or cruise, car rental, etc. Then price each component separately. To get a true picture, be sure to price the exact airline, flight numbers and schedules, room category, etc. If you don't want to invest this kind of time, call your favorite travel agent.

Most vacation packages offer flights from major airports. Every once in a while a great price can be found by checking rates from smaller local airports. Do a Google search for airports and find out which airlines service other area airports. If you're lucky you may find a small, independent airline that may not advertise on major online travel websites. Airlines like Southwest, Allegiant, Frontier and Sun Country can save you a fortune over flights on American or Delta.

Also don't simply take for granted that a round trip-airline ticket will price cheaper than booking two one-way tickets. Recently I needed to make travel arrangements for myself to attend a conference in Las Vegas. Typically, Vegas is a destination that offers plenty of hotel and flight "vacation packages," promising savings to travelers. The casinos will often discount rooms as a way to lure visitors into spending more money in the casinos. I found that I could save $200 by booking my flights and hotel separately instead of booking them as a package. I was also somewhat surprised to find that I could get a much more convenient schedule and save an additional $200 by booking two separate one-way flights instead of one round-trip airline ticket. Hopefully I will be lucky at the craps table too!

Remember a vacation package means a combination of any two or more travel components. Recently I was working with a family from New York that was planning to fly to Miami to stay with Grandma. They wanted my help with flights and a car rental. They also wanted to take a three-night cruise to the Bahamas while they were "in the neighborhood." They also wanted a day trip to swim with the dolphins. It was far less expensive for them to book their flights and car rental as a package and then book their cruise and excursion to swim with the dolphins each separately than it was to book everything as a complete vacation package.

If you're a DIY travel planner, by all means, go online and get pricing. You would be doing yourself a disservice if you didn't at least double-check the best prices you've found with a travel agent. Again, agents work with wholesalers and sources not available to the general public. Many of these companies still maintain discount contracts with airlines and hotels where consumers can still get a bargain by buying a package. Even if you're the winner and you have found a cheaper price online, you can win even more by working with a travel agent. Remember, agents can usually match online discount pricing, but by booking through them you're winning by getting even more customer service, care and expertise.

ALL-INCLUSIVE FAMILY RESORTS

Definition: *A resort where one price includes your family's accommodations, all meals, snacks, drinks (alcoholic and nonalcoholic), resort activities, nightly entertainment, airport transportation, tips and taxes.*

Family all-inclusive resorts are a busy parent's best friend! These resorts provide a kid-friendly atmosphere along with fun activities for every member of the family.

Actually the idea of an all-inclusive vacation began as a solution for honeymooners. Couples wanted a romantic beach resort where they wouldn't have to leave the property. All-inclusive resorts became very popular, but once the honeymooners started having children, the concept for family-friendly resorts was born.

Today there are both adult only and family-friendly all-inclusive resorts. Some resort chains will have both types of resorts sharing the same large piece of property. This is great for situations like destination weddings where the couple wants to invite friends and family with children but prefer to enjoy a more adult atmosphere for their wedding night and honeymoon. With resorts that offer both adult only and family-friendly sections, in many cases adults staying on the family side can enjoy the peace and quiet of the adult side while their kids are happily playing in the kid's club.

In case you're new to the idea of what an all-inclusive resort is about, let's recap. Generally, when you make a reservation at one of these places, the price you pay includes...

- **Hotel room** – Guest rooms that can range from basic accommodations to ultra, luxurious presidential ocean suites. Choice is only limited by your budget.

- **Food** – All your meals and snacks are included. Kid-friendly, all-inclusive resorts offer children's menus and food choices that will please even the pickiest of eaters. Basic all-inclusive properties may just offer a buffet for breakfast, lunch and dinner. Luxury properties may offer dozens of restaurant choices, Michelin-starred chefs and 24 hour room service.

- **Drinks** – All of your drinks are included in the price. Bottled water, soft drinks, coffee, tea... even alcohol for the adults. Parents can enjoy a cocktail at the swim-up bar while kids sip fruit smoothies. Premium wines and liquors are found at high-end properties. Most guest rooms have a mini fridge stocked with water, soft drinks, juices and beer so you won't have to go far if you're thirsty.

- **Daily Entertainment** – All-inclusive resorts offer a plethora of daytime activities like beach sports, dance lessons, nature walks, language lessons, gym work, Karaoke, scavenger hunts, cooking demos and parties. In the evenings there are discos, stage shows, beach parties, dancing and live music. Some resorts even include free sightseeing and scuba diving.

- **Non-Motorized Water Sports** – Any water sport using equipment that does not include a motor. Examples are sailboats, kayaks, snorkeling gear and boogie boards. This equipment is available and free for your family to use without any rental fees. Some all-inclusive, family-friendly resorts even offer elaborate waterparks that are free and part of the all-inclusive program.

- **Gratuities** – Tips are included so you don't have to reach into your pocket every time your family enjoys all that great service.

- **Transportation** – Generally, all-inclusive family resort vacations should also include round-trip airport transportation to get your family from your destination airport to your hotel and back to the airport on your way home. This transportation is called "transfers" in travel industry lingo.

- **Kid's Clubs** – Most all-inclusive family resorts include free child care. Parents know that when the kids are happy and entertained, they are free to relax and enjoy their vacation time too. These kid's clubs are staff-supervised areas that offer fun-filled activities all day long. Games, crafts, sports and cultural activities are offered. Most are open from 9 a.m. to 5 p.m. but some do offer evening group babysitting until 9 p.m. or 10 p.m. Most kid's clubs are for children ranging in age from four to twelve years. There are a few resorts that offer free teen programs and even baby clubs.

Now for a bit of travel industry jargon... family-friendly, all-inclusive resorts can be booked as an all-inclusive VACATION PACKAGE, which includes airfare for your family. For families who want to make their own airline reservations or have plenty of frequent flyer miles, all-inclusive resorts can also be booked as a LAND-ONLY package. A land-only package would mean that your airport transportation and all-inclusive hotel stay would be included in the price.

If you are planning on being your own travel agent and booking your own all-inclusive resort online, be sure to read the fine print to know what you are purchasing. Often round-trip transfers are not included when booking through online websites. This can be a costly mistake upon arrival. It can also mean the risk of dealing with local transportation companies that may or may not be properly insured or held to a high standard of safety.

Often DIY shoppers will proudly tell us how they found a much cheaper price online. Had they taken a moment to study their "great deal" they would realize it comes with strings attached. Often "too good to be true" deals are offered by timeshare sellers. For that cheap price, guests are forfeiting their valuable vacation time to high-pressure sales presentations.

Many parents simply prefer the convenience of booking their all-inclusive resorts with a travel agent. Your agent can book your vacation with or without flights. Other parents may want to use credit card rewards or airline loyalty points towards their flights to help offset the cost of their trip. As mentioned earlier, travel agents don't get any huge economic gains from selling flights so it really doesn't matter either way to them. Most agents will book flights simply as a courtesy or service for their clients. Others may charge a small service fee for their time. An experienced agent will ensure that you have proper airport/hotel transfers with insured and bonded transportation companies with excellent safety records. In addition, many agents have important contacts right in the resort, which can ensure that their clients get preferred dining reservations and other amenities.

The term non-motorized water sports will often confuse people. It basically means any water sports without a motor. Some resorts do require a refundable deposit to ensure that borrowed equipment is returned properly. All you have to do is walk up to the water sports center or dive shop, ask for your equipment and off you go. There would be extra charges for activities like jet skiing, water skiing and diving because these activities include equipment or boats that have motors.

The three reasons why family-friendly, all-inclusive resorts are so popular with parents are:

1. All-inclusive vacations give parents the opportunity to relax and not have to worry about whipping out their wallets every five minutes. No worries about who to tip and how much to give. Want to try some local flavors but not sure if you'll like the taste? Give it a try and if you don't like it, order something else, it's all included. When trying to budget for a vacation, many people tend to underestimate exactly how much things like food, local transportation and activities really cost.

2. All-inclusive resorts take the stress out of day-to-day activities while your family is on vacation. No need to worry about finding good local restaurants, how to get there or what to do all day long. All of these worries have already been taken care of by resort staff. Once again, parents are free to relax and have fun.

3. All-inclusive resorts make it surprisingly easy for parents to budget for their family vacation. Parents know exactly what the total cost of their trip will be up front before they leave home. There is no calculating or "guesstimating" how much everything else is going to cost. No need to fret about next month's credit card bill. The only extras will be souvenirs, items of a personal nature or perhaps a bit of sightseeing.

Most all-inclusive resorts are found in the Caribbean and Mexico. One question frequently asked is... "Why aren't there more all-inclusive family resorts located within the United States?" Honestly, it's a matter of economics. The cost of labor and supplies in the Caribbean and Mexico makes it far more cost-effective and profitable for hotels to operate all-inclusive properties. Operating costs in the United States would make all-inclusive resorts way too expensive for most families to afford.

Many resorts, especially those found in the United States will advertise themselves as being "all-inclusive." Make sure you do your due diligence and compare their definition of all inclusive against the one noted at the beginning of this chapter.

Just about any resort or vacation can be made into a more "all-inclusive" experience. This is done by adding features like a meal plan or child care services. Remember, each of these features comes with an additional price tag. Even a Disney World vacation can be turned into what could be considered an "all-inclusive" vacation by building a package that includes transportation, hotel, meal plans, park admission and even a booze package. You can "get it all" but you will need to "pay for it all."

When selecting an all-inclusive resort or choosing a room in a specific resort, parents need to remember that hotels outside of the United States may have different features. Many foreign hotels do not require elevators in buildings that are three stories or less. This may be an issue for a family member with mobility issues or for parents with young stroller age children. Also, many all-inclusive family resorts will only offer showers in their bathrooms. Bathtubs may not be offered or may only be offered in upgraded room categories.

Some all-inclusive resorts are the size of small cities. Larger resorts offering 2–3,000 rooms will have populations often triple those numbers during busy travel weeks. Because these properties are very spread out, it may mean lots of walking. Larger properties tend to offer golf carts or guest "trains" to help transport guests from their rooms to the pool, beach and other public areas. Guests are free to use this transportation as they need it. Families traveling with very small children or seniors may prefer to opt for a more compact resort that is easier to navigate.

Most all-inclusive resorts offer several dining options that are included in the price you paid for your room. There is a "buffet-style," self-service dining option, which is usually open for breakfast, lunch and dinner. Here families will find a wide variety of quick service choices. Often the food will be "themed" for dinner – Italian, steak night, BBQ, etc., in order to offer variety. In addition to the buffet, there are usually several "*à la carte*" restaurants. Here the phrase "*à la carte*" means waiter service in one of the resort's "specialty" restaurants.

Most all-inclusive resorts offer several different choices of specialty "*à la carte*" restaurants with diverse menu choices... Asian, Italian, Mediterranean, Mexican, etc. Families are escorted to their table and can order whatever they like from the menu, the waiters cater to their every need, and that's it... no tipping and no bill. Guests may be asked their room number or may be asked to sign a receipt, but the meal is free.

Some all-inclusive resorts do not require any dining reservations. Some will require reservations, either in advance or done in the morning for service that evening. Some resorts may have rules regarding the limit of "*à la carte*" dining. For example, if your family is staying for seven nights, they may be allowed reservations to dine in the specialty restaurants four out of the seven nights. The other three nights your family would be required to eat at the buffet.

Many family-friendly, all-inclusive resorts may have an "adults only" restaurant. The kid's club means parents have the opportunity to enjoy a romantic night out without having to cut somebody's meat. Usually this is an upscale French style or steakhouse menu. There may be an additional charge to eat in this type or restaurant. If the restaurant is free and part of the all-inclusive program, there may be an additional fee charged for a specific entrée like lobster, or a specialty bottle of wine. In any case, this would all be clearly noted at the time of making any reservations or on the menu itself.

When choosing a resort, many DIY travel planners will rely on review websites like TripAdvisor to make their final decisions. Guest reviews are certainly one tool to take into consideration. Admittedly, we travel agents keep an eye on these reviews too in order to monitor the quality of resorts. First and foremost remember, not everything you read online is the truth.

Often many of the complaints are written by novice travelers who don't understand the rules. If your room wasn't ready and waiting for you when you arrived at 10 a.m. you probably didn't read the hotel's rules about check-in after 3 p.m. Just because a traveler stated that the beach was full of seaweed in July, it doesn't mean you'll find the same conditions if you plan to visit in February. The resort you're looking to book for the December holidays may have a 92% satisfaction rating but if the construction planned for September isn't completed by the time you arrive, you may not give it the same high rating. Chances are your travel agent will know this but reviewers on TripAdvisor many not be alert to this fact until it's too late.

Just like every family is unique and has its own personality, the same is true with all-inclusive resorts. Some are very loud and active while others are very laid-back and relaxed. Remember there is no one "best" all-inclusive resort out there. What parents are trying to find is the all-inclusive resort that is best suited to the ages, stages and needs of their family, as well as a resort that fits their budget. The perfect resort for a family with a two-year-old might be a nightmare vacation for a family with a 15-year-old. Just as families change, so do resorts. Management and refurbishments change the vibe at a property. This is why our staff frequently visits the resorts that we recommend to our parents. It is important that you work with a travel agent who can offer your family firsthand experience. It's important to work with an agent who to keeps up with all the latest and greatest changes at all the family resorts. This will help your agent play matchmaker... finding the best family all-inclusive resort that perfectly fits the needs, wish list and personality of your family.

Parents who are new to the idea of an all-inclusive resort-style vacation will obviously have lots of questions about the kid's clubs or children's programs they offer. With all-inclusive resorts, their kid's club/child care is complimentary and is included free in the price of your room. That said, each and every all-inclusive resort has its own set of rules regarding age requirements for the kids and their hours of operation. Here are some FAQs we frequently get from parents spending their first vacation at an all-inclusive resort with their kids:

How Old Does My Child Have to Be for the Kid's Club?

The majority of kid's club programs are geared for children ages four-12 years. Children are allowed to attend the kid's club for as much or as little time as they or their parents choose. Depending on the resort, the children's entertainment staff will do their best to arrange activities according to appropriate age groups. For example, during busy spring break week there may be many different activities for several specific age groups due to a high resort population. During slow seasons, all of the children will be required to participate together in all activities.

Some resorts will welcome toddlers ages three and older but will require that those children must be fully potty trained in order to spend time in the kid's club. Staff members here will not change diapers.

There are a few resorts that do offer infant care and/or nannies. Some will allow infants starting from four months of age, while others require babies to be older before they are allowed in the baby care nursery. Staff here will change and feed infants and toddlers under the age of three.

Some resorts will offer a teen club for children 13–17 years of age. Generally, the activities here are not as structured as with younger children. Instead it is a supervised area with video games, snacks and drinks where teens can hang out and interact under the watchful eyes of staff members. More activities may be offered in the evenings like campfires, teen discos and karaoke.

The best kid's clubs keep strict rules. For example, if they say all children must be completely potty trained, they mean it. Please don't expect that your three-year-old who acts very mature will be allowed to stay with their five-year-old sibling if that particular kid's club starts at age four.

How Long Are Your Children Allowed to Be There – Are There Set hours?

Activities, amenities and rules vary with each resort. Some resorts offer everything from personal certified nannies to immense waterparks. Other resorts may advertise that they have a kid's club but, in reality, families will find a tired room with a few videos and board games so you do need to do your homework. Generally, parents get what they pay for, so higher-priced resorts offer more features for the kids to enjoy.

Hours of operation for kid's clubs vary too. Most are open or available seven days a week. Some kid's clubs are open from 9 a.m.–9 p.m. daily; some are just open from 9 a.m. – 5 p.m. Still others may close for an hour or so during the middle of the day. Many resorts will schedule at least one night per week for an evening activity like supervised kids movies by the pool or a campout on the beach so that Mom and Dad can enjoy a romantic dinner alone.

What Type of Activities Will My kids be Doing?

Most kid's club programs have a different schedule of activities each day depending on how many kids are staying in the resort as well as the weather forecast. Typical activities would include:

- Arts and crafts

- Video games, board games, puzzles

- Sports, competitions, scavenger hunts

- Cooking, animal towel folding, resort tours

- Nature walks & garden tours

- Cultural & language lessons

Do You Have to Pre-Book Kids into These Clubs or Just Drop Them Off?

Pre-booking for the kid's club is usually not required. Hotels can tell from their room reservation lists how many children they can expect and will staff accordingly.

If you and your kids are planning on using the kid's club, then your family should check in there shortly after you arrive. Parents are required to visit the resort kid's club and register before their children will be allowed to participate. Normally paperwork is required, which needs to be filled out and signed. Of course, staff will want to know if your child has any special needs, allergies, etc. After that, you can generally just drop kids off. Parents do need to accompany their children to the kid's club and sign them in and out. Some clubs may allow older children to sign themselves in and out, but do require parental signatures for this privilege. Many resorts offer parents cell phones/pagers so they can be easily contacted quickly in case their child needs them.

Some clubs will give parents a list of items to send along with their child each day like sunblock, bathing suits, dry change of clothes, etc. Depending on resort rules, kid's club staff may offer kid-friendly meals in the kid's club or escort children and assist them at the main buffet.

Children are not required to stay for the entire day or any set amount of time. They are welcome to stay for a little or as long as they or their parents choose. There is a list of daily activities – games, crafts, movies, cooking classes, sing-alongs, shows, character visits, etc. Kids may choose to participate in any or all activities.

Do Parents Have to Stay in the Resort or Can They Go Sightseeing?

Parents ARE required to remain on resort property while their children are in the kid's club. Mom and Dad are free go to relax on the beach, schedule a spa treatment, enjoy a great meal or hang out at the pool bar, but they must stay on resort property. Parents ARE NOT allowed leave to the resort to go sightseeing, scuba diving or play a round of golf outside of the resort property.

Some resorts will allow parents to arrange for a one-on-one babysitting for childcare if parents choose to leave the resort. Generally the cost is $20 USD per hour (more if there are multiple kids or if care is late at night). Private babysitting needs to be arranged with the concierge at least 24 hours in advance. Resorts may have safety rules in place as to whether or not babysitters must stay with children in the kid's club area or if they are allowed alone with children in guest rooms.

In conclusion, family-friendly, all-inclusive resorts are an excellent vacation choice offering a good balance of activities for both adults and children. McDonalds, Burger King, White Castle, Five Guys, In-N-Out and Smashburger all sell hamburgers but their brands are distinctly different. The same holds true with the all-inclusive resorts. Every all-inclusive hotel brand has a different level of service, features and list of amenities that they offer to their guests. Besides the different brand features, individual resorts may also reflect different, unique personalities based on their location, local culture, staff and management. The key to a perfect all-inclusive vacation is matchmaking the right resort to the right family.

All-inclusive resorts come with all different price tags. If booked in advance, expect starting prices to be around $100 per person per night plus flights. The higher the price tag, the better the service, food, drinks and amenities. Bear in mind that the cost of doing business is more expensive in some countries than others so, naturally, this too will affect the price you pay. Islands like Aruba or Turks and Caicos will be more expensive to visit than Mexico or the Dominican Republic due to their currency and local labor laws.

FAMILY CRUISES

Did you ever consider driving to the Caribbean? Nearly 75% of all North Americans live within driving distance of one or more of the country's 30 or so cruise ports, according to the Cruise Lines International Association (CLIA). Saving the hassle and the cost of an airline ticket for each person in the family could make an exotic vacation more affordable for many.

The cruise industry is growing faster than just about any other segment of the travel industry, with 26 more ships due to come into service by 2016. The most popular cruise destinations for US families are the Bahamas, Caribbean, Mexico, Alaska, Canada and the Mediterranean. That said, if there is water near your destination, chances are there is a cruise ship that will take you there in style.

A cruise vacation will give your family the opportunity to visit many different destinations and experience several ports of call without the hassle of packing and unpacking. It's a great balance of activities for the entire family. Parents can relax and be pampered while the kids are being engaged and entertained. There are so many great activities onboard for guests of every age and ability making it a great vacation choice for multi-generational vacations and larger groups.

This ain't your grandma's cruise either. Many of today's cruise ships are built specifically with the family market in mind. You'll find features right onboard like waterslides, surf tanks, zip lines, rock climbing, skydiving simulators, skating, 3-D movie theaters, nightly Broadway-style shows, spas, casinos, great food choices and more. There are nurseries for babies right up to teen programs with multiple types of supervised programs like arts, sports, science and more broken down by age-appropriate activities.

In addition to activities offered onboard every ship, families can schedule excursions in each and every port of call they visit (for a fee). Sightseeing, snorkeling, scuba diving, dog sledding, helicopter tours – if you can imagine it, you can enjoy it while on a cruise. Another wonderful cruise feature is that parents can enjoy fun in port with the peace of mind that their little ones are being cared for by trained child care professionals back onboard their ship.

The best part of a cruise vacation is that many of the newer ships have flexible cabin arrangements that can offer more space and togetherness for larger and/or extended families who like to vacation together. Basically there are four choices of cruise ship cabins that determine the price you pay for your cruise:

- Inside cabin – no windows

- Outside cabin – has a window

- Balcony cabin – self-explanatory

- Suites – can go from simply a balcony and more to the most opulent presidential suites with private butlers, grand pianos and enough space to host your own party

Cruise ship cabins offer twin beds that can be joined together for parents. Pack and plays are offered for little ones but again, cruise cabins are small by nature so your room must be able to fit a portable crib. Sleeping arrangements for additional guests sharing the same cabin can vary. There could be a foldout sofa, bunk beds or even upper berths that fold down from the wall. Upper berths may be fun for older kids but a nightmare for parents with toddlers, so be sure to ask about your cabin's specific floor plan.

Family cruises start at around $60 per person per night. Generally the price of your cabin will include all of your meals and snacks, most general shipboard activities, kid's club programs (nurseries will often charge an hourly fee), taxes and port fees. Gratuities generally run approximately $12 per person per day (this includes kids too). This can be added right into the cost of your trip, which most folks prefer.

The biggest difference between a cruise vacation and a resort stay is that most cruise lines charge by the number of guests sharing the same cabin regardless of their age. Usually the first and second passengers sharing the same cabin pay a higher rate (just like double adult occupancy with hotels) but any third, fourth, fifth or additional passengers will pay lower "child" rates. Parents with infants or toddlers will have to pay for that child on a cruise compared to a resort vacation where most of those children often stay for free. Many cruise lines do offer a price break for little ones. On the flip side, this type of pricing structure is a huge bonus for families with teens. If you are parents traveling with a 16-year-old and 19-year-old, both your teens would pay lower "child" rates and you would all be allowed to share the same cabin.

The other nice feature for families onboard a family cruise is that you are allowed to choose, book and confirm your specific cabin(s). This means for parents who want "privacy" or who need space for more kids, that they can have it.

Dining onboard family cruise ships has changed dramatically. It's not all beaded ball gowns and tuxedos. Most cruise lines still offer formal nights. Many families will dress up and take advantage of professional photographers to take family portraits. If that's not your style, cruise lines offer families all sorts casual of dining options and kid-friendly menus. Most ships do offer main dining room reservations each night but your family is not forced to eat there. You can opt for a quick buffet meal or room service if you've had a busy day of fun. Many of the newer ships offer recognizable restaurants onboard like Starbucks, Johnny Rockets and even gourmet dining from celebrity chefs. Often these dining options do come with a surcharge, which will be clearly noted or you can just ask.

As far as beverages go, most cruise lines will offer coffee, tea, ice tea and water in all of their restaurants... booze and usually soda cost extra. Soda service generally costs $5–$6 per day plus 15% tip and this includes a refillable, thermos-style cup. When it comes to alcohol, wine and beer, these can be purchased at the bar for a cost comparable to a moderate restaurant. Many of the cruise lines are now offering add-on packages for alcohol to make cruises more of an all-inclusive experience.

All of the major family cruise lines have aligned themselves with different entertainment partners. This means characters, movies, parades and experiences are onboard for kids of all ages. Obviously there are Disney movies and character photo ops onboard Disney ships. Royal Caribbean is partnered with Universal and Dreamworks. The "n" in Norwegian also stands for the Nickelodeon characters onboard. Carnival recently announced a partnership with Dr. Seuss.

Cruising with Baby

Do bear in mind that the cruise lines have policies and rules in place regulating what age babies are allowed onboard cruise ships, just as they have rules for pregnant moms. Even though all cruise ships have a medical unit staffed with doctors and nurses for medical emergencies, they endeavor to prevent risking the health of passengers. These rules have been established for the comfort and safety of all passengers, and the cruise lines do strictly enforce these rules. Most cruise lines restrict pregnant moms onboard during their final trimester. Every cruise line is different so do check with your travel agent for specifics.

Disney Cruise Line – is the winner when it comes to baby cruises. Disney Cruise Lines will allow infants as young as 12 weeks on the day of embarkation to sail on their ships. Group babysitting is available for children 12 weeks to three years old at Flounder's Reef Nursery on the Disney Magic and the Disney Wonder. The Disney Dream offers baby care at their "It's a Small World" nursery. There is an hourly charge for this service. It is not free like the kid's clubs offered onboard for older children. Parents will be given a pager as the nursery staff here do not change diapers for health reasons. The ratio of care givers to children is 1:4 for infants and 1:6 for toddlers.

Carnival Cruise Line – sets their minimum sailing age for babies at six months, with the exception of Transatlantic, Hawaii and South American Cruises, which require infants to be at least one year of age. Children younger than two can play with the toys during designated family play times in the "Camp Carnival" areas, but parents must be present at all times. There are babysitting services available during limited hours for children younger than two at "Camp Carnival" for an additional fee.

Royal Caribbean International - requires infants sailing on a cruise to be at least six months old as of the first day of the cruise/cruise tour. However, for Transatlantic, Transpacific, Hawaii, certain South American sailings and other selected cruises, infants must be at least 12 months old at the time of embarkation. "Royal Babies & Tots" nursery program is available on certain ships and offers supervised care for little ones ages 6–36 months. Daytime and evening drop-off is offered for an hourly fee. In addition, Royal Caribbean also offers scheduled interactive playgroups where little ones can come to the nursery and play while in the company of their parents.

Norwegian Cruise Line – Infants must be six months of age on the first day of sailing. If the itinerary contains three to four consecutive sea days then infants must be 12 months old to sail. No private or in-stateroom babysitting is available on any NCL vessel. Norwegian does offer their "Splash Academy for Guppies" for children ages six months to three years, with daily activities for babies, but parents must be present at all times.

MSC Cruises – Infants must be six months of age to sail. Group baby care is offered from 1–2 p.m. and 6–7 p.m. in the kid's club for a fee. Playgroup time for babies is also offered in the kid's club but all children must be accompanied by an adult. No in-cabin babysitting is offered.

Princess Cruises – has a minimum sailing age of six months. There are parent-supervised under two " Zooplay" areas onboard. After-hours group babysitting is available for a fee for kids older than two. In-cabin private babysitting is not offered.

Holland America Line – will not accept reservations for infants younger than six months of age at the time of sailing. For trans-ocean crossings or other itineraries that their medical department staff feel present a significant risk, infants must be a minimum of 12 months at embarkation. No babysitting services are offered for children under the age of three or for children not yet potty trained.

Fearless Family Vacations

Cunard Line– requires children to be one year of age to sail, however, certain sailings will allow infants six months and older. They have certified British nannies onboard to care for babies age one and older in supervised nurseries with baby toys and cribs. Children must be a minimum of one year old to participate in the children's programs without parental supervision. On specific sailings, children between the ages of six months and one year are welcome in the children's centre to play, provided they are accompanied by a parent/guardian at all times. Private babysitting is not available. However, complimentary child sitting on a group basis is available in the evenings.

Please know that the cruise lines are very strict about their age restrictions and policies towards babies. This is done for the safety and comfort of all passengers. Misrepresenting the age of your child is not allowed. At embarkation, if cruise officials check your child's passport or birth certificate and determine your baby to be underage, the infant and their guardian will NOT be allowed to board the ship. This is called "denied boarding." It is not covered by any travel insurance, and you will simply forfeit the cost of your cruise.

Generally speaking, parents using nursery services at sea will find that there are a few standard procedures. Registration and initial paperwork will need to be filled out on the first day giving details of your child's preferences and any special care or dietary needs. Parents must also bring all necessary gear with them including food, formula, diapers, wipes, sunscreen and changes of clothing. These items are not provided for your baby while in the nursery. Liability waivers will also need to be signed in accordance with the rules. Parents will be familiarized with the rules and procedures of the facility. Remember, if you are not present to pick up your child at the appropriate time or choose not to respect the rules of the nursery, you will either be charged a fee or your baby will not be eligible to participate. Once again, strict rules are in place to protect the health and safety of all children and staff.

Cruise cabins are generally small by nature. Take square footage into consideration when pricing your cabin and consider spending a few dollars more to upgrade to a stateroom that offers a bit more space. Once again, use off-season rates to your advantage. Often the cost difference will offset the cost of an upgrade making your cruise more comfortable for all. Leave your huge Cadillac of jogging strollers at home and opt for a collapsible umbrella stroller for the cruise.

Another consideration when cruising with baby is a bathtub. Most cruise ships only offer showers in their lower-category cabins like inside or ocean view. Depending on the ship, you may need to upgrade to a balcony or suite to get a bathroom that offers a bathtub. If an upgrade doesn't work for your budget even in off-season, consider packing a small inflatable baby pool or tub to make bath time a bit easier.

Speaking of baby gear, it's easy enough to pack the trunk of your car with diapers and formula if your family will be driving to port prior to your cruise. If your family needs to fly to get to port, then packing diapers and formula really isn't practical. Most of the family-friendly cruise lines either offer or partner with services that will deliver diapers, formula, baby food, wipes and any other items you may need straight to your cabin. Ask your travel agent and plan ahead as time is required prior to departure to place your orders and have them delivered. It's best to order your baby items about one month in advance to avoid any extra last-minute air shipping charges. Keep track of how much formula your baby uses in a week and how many diapers. It's recommended to order approximately 25% more than average use, just to ensure you're not caught short.

Cruise ships have self-service pay laundry facilities available for all guests. Individual packets of detergent are available. If your child has allergies to certain laundry products, consider bringing a Ziploc bag of your usually laundry powder along.

Like some of the all-inclusive resorts, the family-friendly cruise lines also offer playgroups or baby care. Each cruise line has its own policies and the rules and services may vary between ships. Here is a list of the most family-friendly cruise lines and their rules and policies regarding cruising with babies...

Cruising with Toddlers

Disney Cruise Line – Toddlers over the age of three can enjoy plenty of Disney fun while onboard in the Oceaneer's Club and Lab. Toddlers must be potty trained to participate in the program. Disney offers a plethora of fully supervised, age-appropriate activities including arts and crafts, dress up and even character meets. Parents can leave children in the care of the Oceaneer Club on port days. Disney also provides a kid's club on their private Caribbean island called Castaway Cay. Evening programs are also available for an additional fee.

Carnival Cruise Lines – Camp Carnival allows children as young as two years of age to participate in their fully supervised program. Counselors will change diapers but parents must provide all gear. Camp Carnival is open during port days and parents are allowed to leave their children in the program while they are in port or on excursions. There are evening babysitting services available for an additional fee.

Royal Caribbean International – Once your tot reaches age three, they are allowed to participate in Royal Caribbean's Ocean Adventure club. Children age three to five are allowed to participate in complimentary, fully supervised, age-appropriate activities throughout the day. All "Aquanauts" must be fully potty trained and pull up free. Fisher-Price, Crayola and Dreamworks are all partners, so many of their activities for this age-group center around these themes. Daytime and evening drop-off babysitting and even in-cabin babysitting is offered for an hourly fee.

Norwegian Cruise Line – NCL offers their complimentary, fully supervised Turtle program for children starting at age three up to age five. Fun, age-appropriate activities are offered throughout the day, including visits from kids' favorite Nickelodeon characters at sea. Toddlers do not have to be potty trained but staff will not change diapers. Parents are notified when diapers need changing and must appear with the appropriate gear to do the deed. For this reason, at least one parent must remain onboard during port days when your toddler participates in the Turtle program. No private or in-stateroom babysitting is available on any NCL vessel.

MSC Cruises – To participate in MSC's kids' programs children must be 3 years old and potty trained. MSC Cruises offers a new MSC Baby Care Services for children 1 to 3 years old. It is available when the ship is at sea for limited times. They will change diapers.

Princess Cruises – The Princess Pelican Club offers complimentary, supervised kid's club activities for children age three to five. All children must be fully potty trained to attend. Children under the age of three and/or those not yet potty trained are welcome but must be accompanied by a parent at all times. After-hours group babysitting is available for an additional fee but no in-cabin babysitting is offered.

Holland America Line – Club HAL is open on sea days only to potty trained kids, starting at age three. Port day programs are available with special registration and an additional free. Babysitting services are available from 10 p.m. until 12 midnight at Club HAL. After-hours babysitting is available for children age three and older.

Cunard Line– Toddlers are part of the one- to six-year-old set onboard Cunard ships. Free child care onboard starts from one year old and up with certified British nannies, and staff here will change diapers. Because this is a luxury line there are generally less children onboard so more attention is given by staff. Complimentary child sitting on a group basis is available in the evenings on a first-come, first-served basis.

Swim Diapers

Some cruise lines allow them, some don't, and for others it depends on the specific ship. Many of the newer ships will have a small, splash play area for babies and toddlers who are not yet potty trained and are using swim diapers. These areas have their own filtration system separate from the other pools onboard.

They can easily be drained, disinfected and properly cleaned to prevent the spread of germs.

Disney – Swim diapers are allowed on all their ships.

Royal Caribbean – offer splash zones on newer ships and many of their older ships are adding this feature as ships are dry docked for upgrades.

Carnival, Norwegian, Princess, Cunard, MSC and Holland America – do not allow swim diapers. Many will allow parents to bring a small inflatable baby pool to entertain little ones on deck but water must be disposed of by staff.

Kid's Clubs, Tweens and Teens

Most of the kid's programs are open during the daytime hours. Evening babysitting programs offered at the kid's clubs are available for parents of younger kids for an additional fee. Tween and teen programs tend to open later in the morning and may run into the wee hours. There are a few major differences between resort kid's clubs and the kid's activities offered by the cruise lines. Again, volumes could be written here about every detail and activity onboard every ship. Rules, activities and features are often updated and frequently change as older ships are updated and new ships sail into service. This is where your travel agent can guide you on all of the specifics for the cruise that is "best" for your family.

With resort kid's clubs, most offer activities for ages four to twelve years. The entertainment staff will supervise and organize activities based on the ages of the kids for that day. Your four-year-old might be trying to keep up with a group of 10-year-olds. On the cruise ships there are separate and fully staffed areas for each different age-group. The kid's club staff on cruise ships must have a degree in education or child care. Age-groups are basically broken down by every two years: 3–5, 6–8, 9–11, 12–14, 15–17. This means your kids will be making friends and interacting with peers of their own age. The cruise ships are usually strict about siblings of different age-groups wanting to be together, so please do not expect your five-year-old to be allowed to play with his/her nine-year-old sibling.

Few resorts offer teen programs. If there is a teen program, most likely your 13-year-old will be mingling with 17-year-olds. Family cruise ships all offer teen programs and, once again, they are very age-specific. Having fully supervised evening activities like karaoke, video game competitions and dance parties will help them to make new friends and have more fun. For teens "too cool" to hang with their parents, many cruise lines offer specific, supervised shore excursions just for teens (for a fee).

Another nice feature of a cruise vacation is the limited independence it offers for older kids and teens. Newer ships offer bracelets with GPS chips so parents can go to the nearest touch screen and see exactly where their kids are onboard the ship at any given moment. Ship ID cards are needed to order drinks so this deters underage kids from being served alcohol. Ship ID cards can also be allotted with a daily spending limit (or none at all) so parents can control funds.

Besides all the kid's club activities, cruise ships offer tons of other daily activities that families of all ages can enjoy doing together. Trivia games, mini golf, ping pong, dance competitions, classes of all sorts or even just relaxing by the pool all offer a chance for families to come together while having fun. Having the opportunity to visit and explore so many different ports of call and have new experiences together will certainly create years' worth of memories to share.

ESCORTED TOURS

Mention an escorted or guided tour and many folks picture a bunch of senior citizens on a bus ride to look at fall leaves or a fast walking, flag carrying guide in Paris followed by a group of tourists with cameras flashing away like paparazzi.

In recent years, the travel industry has wised up to the opportunity of creating guided tours with itineraries especially designed for families. Long respected tour companies like Tauck, Collette and Abercrombie & Kent now offer family tours – even Adventures by Disney was created with specific guided, escorted tours to some of the most fascinating spots in the world. Most importantly, these itineraries cater specifically to the needs of families with kids. Some companies even offer specific departure dates for families with kids of certain ages like teen only tours.

Think Paris, Rome, Australia, US national parks, the Great Wall of China and Peru's Machu Picchu, all exciting experiences, with itineraries geared for a family's enjoyment Guided tours mean parents can be participants in their OWN vacations. There are no worries about logistics, where to go, how to get there, getting ripped off – your tour guide handles everything. Imagine a guided tour and wine tasting at a vineyard in Italy while your kids are supervised picking and stomping grapes.

Family escorted tours do have recommended age requirements for participating kids. Some tours will allow younger children and others will not. If your children are excluded due to age, please do not take it personally. Tour companies need to ensure that all of their guests have a fun and enjoyable time. Some family tours may have very specific age requirements on specific departure dates for the same tour or destination. For example, there may be specific tours to a destination with activities created just for teens. Be sure to talk to your travel agent, read the fine print and be aware of these requirements.

Escorted tours will initially appear expensive "on paper." One point to bear in mind is that on an escorted tour, you are sharing the cost of the services offered by your guide. Many would consider having an experienced person(s) at your side to manage, facilitate, drive, teach and guide your family on vacation as priceless. Your guide's knowledge and insights can greatly enhance your family's overall vacation enjoyment and ultimate experience.

Again, folks often fail to fairly calculate the travel math. Each and every tour will offer different "inclusions." When comparing your options, make sure you are comparing "apples to apples." Some tours will include meals, tips, admissions and entrance fees. If your tour does not, you'll need to research what these additional costs will be in order to determine the best value between two tours. Some tour companies will offer stays in luxury hotels with ideal locations and top-of-the-line amenities. Other tours will offer a clean place to sleep for the night. Normally the higher the price tag, the more priceless the experience.

Many folks think they can save money by putting together individual components of a similar trip online themselves. Often they are surprised at the results.

Tour companies get volume discounts from hotels and transportation companies. They also get perks and experiences like after-hours access to the Vatican, for example. This type of access can save hours of waiting in line with the crowds. Many use their clout and reputation to create "once-in-a-lifetime experiences" which money just can't buy. Sure, anyone can plan a trip to California and Disneyland. When your family takes an Adventures by Disney escorted tour, you get to visit Skywalker Ranch to see how George Lucas creates Star Wars movies. You will get to visit Walt and his family's personal apartment on Main Street USA, as well as all the Disneyland rides. The takeaway difference here is the experience.

Escorted family tours like this are offered throughout the year but particularly during the summer months and school holidays. Specific departure dates are set in advance. It's not like a hotel where a family can arrive and start their vacation any day they choose.

With an escorted tour your travel dates are set in stone. Your family must be at the destination and ready to meet with your group at a set time and date to start your adventure.

Remember, when traveling with a group, the group waits for no one. This means they will leave without you and you will forfeit the cost of your outing or you will be responsible to pay any additional travel costs in order to catch up with your group. This is why it is extremely wise to arrive at your group departure destination at least one day prior to the start of your escorted tour. If your family will be flying more than five hours to reach the starting point of your tour, jet lag may become an issue. In this case, parents may want to consider adding additional "pre-tour" days so that everyone is well rested and ready to start their big adventure.

Tour companies have calculated their costs and profits by the number of participants they have on every tour. Found in the "fine print" of most escorted tour contracts is a minimum number of guests per tour. For example, let's say the contracted minimum for a given tour is 16 and only 12 people sign up to go, the tour company has the right to cancel that tour or to combine it with another comparable departure. If your family has already purchased your airline tickets or if this is the only date your family can travel, this can be a costly and disappointing situation. This is why you want to try to find a tour with a "guaranteed departure." This means either that the tour already has enough participants or the tour company will go ahead with the tour regardless of the number of participants.

Some tour companies will also book your flights for an additional fee and they will be responsible for any cancellation costs if a tour does not meet a minimum number of participants. In many cases, flight choices through the tour companies are limited and more expensive. Parents may also choose to arrange their own flights using credit card or airline loyalty points. Travel agents also can help with access to overseas flight discounts. Again, it is important to be covered by the correct travel insurance to protect yourself and your vacation investments.

Accommodations for larger families may be an issue for some destinations. For example, older hotel buildings in Europe often have much smaller rooms than American tourists are accustomed to back home. Cheaper tours offering tourist class hotels may only offer double occupancy rooms. If you are a family of four you will be required to pay for two rooms and there is a good chance your kids will pay adult rates. More expensive tours may offer luxury hotels that will offer suites for larger families and may surprisingly end up being a better value because your kids paying child rates.

Referring back to our earlier discussion on travel personalities, if your family members are outgoing, touristy or adventure types who enjoy meeting new people, then an escorted tour is a perfect choice for your vacation. Parents or grandparents with shy kids or those traveling with only one child also really appreciate these types of touring vacations. Tour guides are skilled in bringing everyone together. With an escorted tour, your family will be on the move, see a great deal of territory and experience many fun new adventures. Each day will be structured according to a timetable and schedule. If you appreciate flexibility, independence and serendipity then this style of vacation may not be your best choice.

Escorted tours are not just confined to land travel. Many cruise companies are offering a "combination vacation." For example, you can take a cruise to Alaska and then journey by rail or bus into Denali National Park with a professional tour guide. Sail the Mediterranean to see the capitals of Europe while your tour guide takes the family on a fascinating tour of discovery in each port of call you visit.

If you have enough people in your family, many tour companies will create a custom group itinerary just for you. Each tour company has their own magic number when it comes to their definition of a "private group." Some luxury tours may require as few as 10 passengers. Others may require 25–30 guests before they will create a custom tour. Often these rules are determined by logistics like how many passengers can fit in a minibus that can navigate narrow cobblestone streets in Europe.

If your family has always talked about visiting Ireland to see where Grandma and Grandpa were born, a customized tour may be the easiest way to make this dream a reality. As we discussed in early chapters, group discounts will most likely apply so the more, the merrier.

THEME PARKS

Theme park vacations come in every shape and size. They are found in just about every corner of the globe. There are some generalized tips to follow no matter which park you plan to visit...

Theme parks tend to offer something to suit travelers of every age. Some parks are better than others at offering baby care stations or toddler attractions but, overall, it's a great option for blended and extended families of all different ages.

Just be mindful when traveling with very young infants/toddlers or seniors, especially those with mobility or health issues. This is not a time to be cheap. Rent strollers or scooters, make sure everyone stays well hydrated and spend the extra money for accommodations close to or in the park.

- Theme park vacations tend to be a bit pricier than say a week at the beach because you are paying a higher premium here to be entertained. Parents will pay park admission in addition to any travel and accommodation costs. Often "adult" prices start at a much lower age. Don't be surprised to learn your nine-year-old is considered a full paying adult.

- The longer you stay, the better the price you'll get on the cost of admission to the parks. However, the longer you stay the more you will pay for accommodations and food, so do your travel math.

- Food inside the parks is very pricey because hungry park guests are a captive audience. In order to save, BYOP (Bring Your Own Picnic) if you are allowed. If you plan to stay for a couple days, consider a food plan if it is offered. It may seem expensive on paper but will no doubt save you in the long run.

- When kids are out on school holidays, theme parks will be more crowded. This means longer lines and fewer opportunities to go on rides. If you're not tied to a school calendar, by all means take advantage of less crowded times like early September, May or December when you can also take advantage of lower prices.

- Do your homework, get a map and have a plan before you leave home. If you have young children, research any ride restrictions for height or age. This may save aggravation, time and disappointments. Prioritize "must-see" attractions and know how to find them in the park. This is especially important if you're traveling during busy times. Most parks now have smartphone apps that can help you purchase tickets, see line wait times, park hours, maintenance schedules, find your parking spot and many more features to make your park visit more enjoyable.

- Take a photo of everyone and a photo of where you parked your car. Just in case you get separated from your children, you'll have a current photo along with a clothing description to pass along to park security. Ensuring you have a reminder of your parking spot can be a lifesaver after a very long and tiring day of fun.

- Prep your kids in advance on topics like expected behavior, the time you'll be spending in the park, meals, souvenir shopping budgets, etc. Again, if everyone knows the rules of engagement in advance, it will leave less for discussion in the heat of the moment.

Disney

Walt Disney took the idea of a typical amusement park and created a phenomenon beyond the wildest imagination of many. The Disney name is not only the granddaddy of all theme parks and a leader in the hospitality industry, but also THE global entertainment and media brand. For all of these reasons it has become the Magical Mecca for family vacations for a few generations.

As of 2013, the company's theme parks in the United States, Paris, Tokyo, Hong Kong and Shanghai hosted approximately 132.5 million guests, making Disney parks the world's most visited theme park company.

Despite its worldwide popularity and its mention in numerous guidebooks and online references, surprisingly many parents are often not familiar with some of the basics when it comes to planning a visit to a Disney theme park...

- **Disneyland** – is located in Southern California. The original park was built and dedicated by Walt Disney himself on July 17, 1955. Disneyland will celebrate its diamond anniversary in 2015, and has welcomed over 650 million visitors through its gates over the years. It was built on 160 acres in Anaheim, California just south of Los Angeles. In 2001, a second theme park was added. There was a 72 acre expansion with the addition of Disney California Adventure Park adjacent to the original Disneyland Park.

- **Walt Disney World Resort (also known as Walt Disney World or Disney World)** – is located near Orlando, Florida. It was opened in 1971 shortly after Walt Disney died in 1966. By contrast, Walt Disney World covers close to 30,000 acres (about 45 square miles). It offers four different theme parks – the Magic Kingdom, Epcot, Disney Hollywood Studios and Disney's Animal Kingdom. In addition, there are over 25 "in-the-park" themed resort hotels, two water parks, four golf courses, campgrounds, shopping district and many more entertainment venues. Attendance at Walt Disney World Resort tops 50 million visitors every year. *(Note: Harry Potter is found at Universal Studios in Orlando and not at any Disney park).*

A quick glance at these stats proves how different it is to plan a family vacation to Disneyland California versus Walt Disney World Florida. Disneyland and California Adventure are easy to walk and navigate. Families can enjoy just about every single attraction these parks have to offer within three to four days. By comparison, Disney World Orlando is about the size of Manhattan. Families need to surrender to the fact that they will never be able to see everything during a one-week vacation.

For families planning a Disney vacation in either Florida or California the news is both good and bad. Families can visit either Disneyland or Disney World on a tight budget or they can be as extravagant as a princess. Either way, they can look forward to enjoying a fantastic vacation experience. The bad news is, because there are so very many different choices when it comes to a Disney park vacation, it often makes it tricky for many parents to find the "best" option for their family. This can make vacation planning a bit confusing and overwhelming.

To add to all of these choices, Disney is constantly evolving and offering new innovations. New rules, new attractions, new dining, new magic bands – we travel professionals spend hours updating our training and visiting the parks just to keep up with everything new at Disney. (I appreciate that this last statement sounds like great fun but when we visit, we are working, gathering facts, attending training sessions, passing tests... it's not a "walk in the park").

Whether spending a little or a lot, every family wants to get the most fun out of their vacation time together. Every parent also wants to get the most "bang for their vacation buck." In order to achieve this goal, Disney vacations take proper planning.

There are those parents and novice travelers who will not heed this warning. You'll see these glassy-eyed, arguing parents wandering aimlessly around the parks with gaping mouths and cranky kids. On the flip side are the Disney cultists standing ready to sprint when the park opens at rope drop with organized binders and a detailed itinerary that would put most military maneuvers to shame. Once again, balance is the key. Most families will find themselves somewhere in the middle of these two extremes with a thoughtful plan that allows time for fun, rest and lots of magical "seren-dipity-doh-dah."

Once again, a travel agent with specialized Disney training can help you far beyond flights and hotels. In order to get reservations for certain Disney restaurants and character dining experiences, there is a timeline that needs to be followed depending on your choice of hotel. A good travel agent will take care of all of this for you. This way you won't need to take the time out of your busy day to hang on hold (sometimes for hours listening to "It's a Small World") to make reservations. A good Disney agent will watch for sales and have lower prices applied to your existing reservations when applicable. The same holds true for things like "free dining" perks.

Most importantly, your travel agent can suggest a daily touring itinerary. Combining Extra Magic Hours, park event schedules, phone apps, dining reservations and fast passes means more fun for your family with less waiting in line.

Orlando versus California (Less Is More)

Where there are Disney theme parks, families will find plenty of other theme parks and attractions in the nearby area. In Orlando you have Universal Studios, SeaWorld, Busch Gardens and Legoland. In Southern California you have Universal Studios Hollywood, SeaWorld, San Diego Zoo, Knott's Berry Farm and Legoland.

Excited and enthusiastic families planning for a fun-filled vacation will want to "do it all." Not only will this be an expensive venture but often a recipe for disappointment. Novice travelers often neglect the distance and traffic between all these parks. They fail to appreciate the crowds in the parks during school holidays. Travel time and logistics will cut into their time enjoying the park itself. Considering the cost of park admission, every minute inside the park truly counts.

Your energy and excitement levels will be high as your plan your trip but after a few full days in the park, you may begin to question your own sanity. Family vacation planning is a very delicate balance of quality vs. quantity. Remember this is your vacation, not a marathon of endurance. Devote the proper time to your priorities and the "must see" attractions on your list. This way you won't return home needing a vacation from your recent vacation.

If "money is not object" then your family can afford to purchase "VIP passes," that allow you to be escorted through the parks and skip every line. With this option, you will cover more ground but you still won't be able to see everything in one trip. Use the answers to your six travel questions to find the appropriate options for your family. Maybe this means a visit to one park this year and a return to the same location next year to see other parks. Maybe Mom and the little ones spend a day at one park while Dad takes your tween to visit their favorite in another park. Compromise and balance is the key to getting the most out of your family's theme park vacation.

FAMILY ADVENTURE VACATIONS

Hiking, biking, camping, going on safaris, skiing, horseback riding, repelling, surfing, zip lining... you name the adventure and your family's vacation can be structured around your favorite interest.

Once again, the key to planning any successful adventure vacation for your family is to ensure that there are activities geared to the appropriate age and abilities of each and every traveler. Information and education is paramount when it comes to the safety and enjoyment of everyone.

Of course you've gone through the six guideline steps and have decided you want a taste of adventure. One additional, very important question you must truthfully answer is, "What is your level of adventure expertise and what abilities do all family members possess?"

Families need to take an honest reality check of experience, expertise, health and abilities of everyone who plans to partake in this vacation adventure. Are your family experienced adventurers or do you simply think this would be a fun type of vacation to try? Some kids have the skills to fly airplanes by themselves or navigate a boat like an adult. Other kids are video game adventurers aboard the living room sofa. Someone who runs five miles on the beach every morning may still not be able to handle a three-day climb of the Inca Trail to Machu Picchu at 12,000 feet elevation.

An honest assessment of your family's skills will also you determine whether this adventure vacation is something your family can do by themselves or whether it would be best to travel with others as part of a group or with the help of a teacher or guide. Planning a ski trip for a family of experts will be far different than a ski vacation for a family who have never been skiing before. Perhaps your family has enjoyed biking through France. You may have planned all of these details yourself and feel confident about taking a bike tour in Vietnam. However, leftover land mines in some areas of Vietnam may mean it would be more prudent to be part of a guided tour or at least to hire an experienced guide for this year's biking vacation.

An adventure vacation doesn't necessarily mean a week's stay in the wilderness foraging for critters and berries for supper. There are African safaris that offer "glamping," luxury tents complete with private butler service and gourmet dining. Many luxury vacations and high-end escorted tours can offer a few days of adventure activities while staying in some of the finest accommodations. A family cruise will offer enjoyment for everyone, as well as child care for the kids, allowing Mom and Dad the opportunity to zip line or hike a glacier while the ship is in port. Adventure travel doesn't have to be an "all or nothing" proposition. It can be worked into any itinerary for families that require balance and some compromise in order to keep everyone happy.

Specialized sports equipment is often necessary for adventure vacations. If everyone in the family needs their own equipment in order to participate, this may mean a lot of extra baggage. If your family needs to fly to their adventure destination, you'll need to consider the extra costs involved. Not only will everyone need to pay for their airfare but there will be extra costs for shipping items like bikes, skis, surfboards or scuba gear. Double-check luggage size requirements and oversize fees in advance so that you're not shocked at the airport.

Equipment may be another good reason to work with an adventure tour operator. Many guides or escorted tours include the use of equipment. Any type of gear that you may need will be ready, set and waiting for you to use. This is not only a tremendous convenience but depending on the specifics, it can be cheaper than schlepping all of your own gear from home. If you are traveling overseas, specific countries may have very specialized gear or rules requiring the need to use very specialized equipment.

Safety is every family's priority. Even if your entire family is very experienced regarding a specific activity, local destination knowledge is also a factor when it comes to keeping everyone safe and healthy. It is important to not only work with a guide but to work with an experienced and very reputable one. Working local knowledge of terrain, equipment, flora, fauna and customs can not only add to your overall experience but, in some circumstances, help your family avoid danger.

Many reputable tour and guide companies are members of USTOA –United States Tour Operators Association. Members of USTOA offer tours and guides at just about every destination around the world. The USTOA motto is "integrity in tourism," and it requires members to adhere to the highest standards in the industry. Among these is the principle of ethical conduct, which requires members to conduct business according to a set of professional standards which include representing all facts, conditions and requirements. Travel agents know why it is important to work with reputable tour companies and guides. Sadly many novice travelers or DIY planners simply consider the price of the trip. This type of vacation planning can be a recipe for disaster.

Adventure travel is all about the fun getting that adrenalin rush. Extreme activities usually involve an added element of risk as part of that adventure. Parasailing, rock climbing or spending a few hours up close and personal with gorillas in Africa inherently means more risk for your family compared to spending a week at the beach building sand castles. For this reason, typical travel insurance will not cover you or your family if you plan to partake in any adventures they would deem as being "risky." For an insurance company, increased risk means increased costs. Be aware that there are separate travel insurance policies that do cover extreme sports or adventure vacations along with all of their activities.

Many tour companies that arrange adventure vacation packages and guided tours do offer travel insurance for an additional fee. In most cases, this insurance will cost more than typical travel insurance because adventure travelers have an increased risk of injury. Having this convenience is yet another reason to go with a reputable adventure tour company or escorted tour. If you are a DIY travel planner, be sure that you do include the right kind if travel insurance and make sure your coverage will protect you for the specific activities you plan to enjoy on your vacation.

Remember, even if you are planning on a week at the beach or a seven-day cruise but plan on taking a one-day excursion to rock climb down a waterfall, make sure you have the right type of insurance coverage to enjoy that day trip free from worry. If not, should you find yourself injured, you may find yourself paying out of pocket for any medical care or transportation back home.

Some destinations are best seen as part of an adventure. The majesty of the Rocky Mountains, the Grand Canyon or the coastline of Maine can be best appreciated through our national parks. It would seem foolish to fly all the way to Africa simply to stay in a hotel. Africa speaks to your heart by interacting with its people, its culture and experiencing animals in the wild. Families who hike the Nepali coastline of Kauai will return with a completely different memory of Hawaii compared to the tourists of Oahu. Family adventure travel isn't right for every family, but for those families who do enjoy a walk on the wild side, they will share a world of very unique memories.

« Final Note »

"Twenty years from now you will be more disappointed by the things you didn't do than by the ones you did do." – Mark Twain

Changing your family's normal daily experiences will certainly have a tremendous positive effect on everyone's attitude. Traveling forces all of us to stretch our limits and to break internal boundaries. It helps us to celebrate the best in one another. Travel experiences tie families together in a way that is unlike anything else we encounter. Most of us can't remember what we did yesterday but most of us can still remember the family vacations we took as a kid.

The laughter of children is more precious than gold. I hope this book will enable many more parents to become extremely wealthy with that joy while sharing priceless memories with their kids.

Nobody can look into the future. Tomorrow is promised to no one. Memories are ours to keep, even when the going gets a bit rough. For this reason, I urge every parent not to dream and wish about a vacation but to take action and plan. You cannot go back and change yesterday.

In hindsight, there is a regret I do have regarding my own family vacations. It came to light as I was writing this book. I wish I had done a much better job recording and journaling all of our vacations together.

Often a return from a family vacation means "catch-up" time for busy parents. We need to catch up on work we missed, the kids' school work, laundry, food shopping and more. We return home to a whirlwind of activities precisely when our vacation memories are fresh in our minds.

I would urge parents to make the time to organize photos and write down our thoughts. Even if this means adding a day onto a vacation, I would certainly schedule the time to make this a priority. I would record and edit little interviews of my kids before, during and after our trip. It's a great activity that encourages participation from every member of the family. Your creativity is only limited by your imagination. If you need a bit of inspiration, you'll find plenty these days on Pinterest.

Even if I didn't have the time to do this I would hire someone to organize, edit, scrapbook and archive these precious memories for posterity. Help can be found on websites like Fiverr or Elance.

I hope you have found this book to be helpful, encouraging and insightful. This was my goal when I sat down to write it. I do hope it has sparked ideas and answered many of your family travel questions.

Please know I welcome hearing your thoughts, feedback and suggestions. I enjoy connecting and chatting with folks about their vacations.

I wish you all photo frames, albums and hearts filled with smiles and warm, loving vacation memories along with wishes for years of happy travels together.   ~Sally

www.Vacationkids.com

610-681-7360

mom@vacationkids.com

www.Facebook.com/Vacationkids

www.Twitter.com/Vacationkids

Made in the USA
Middletown, DE
30 September 2016